3

Acknowledgements

Cornwall County Record Office for the Will of Degory Baron AP/B/1905/1, and Inventory AP/B/1905/2, and other help.

Public Record Office for the Tregeare Accounts (1800) C/38/1003 p.91, for Court Report extract C/33/560 page 97 and for the Will of Jasper Baron PROB 10/3452.

Ordnance Survey for extracts from 1st Edition 1884 and 2nd Edition 1906 maps, and extract from Edition B Pathfinder 1326.

Mr. Christopher Lethbridge for the portraits of Elizabeth Ann Baron, Christopher and Polly Lethbridge, Baron and Millicent Lethbridge, and others.

Mr. Richard Lethbridge for the portraits of Jasper Baron, William and Elizabeth Ann, and Oliver (or William) Baron, and others.

Mrs. Dorothy Lloyd for her portrait of Jasper Baron.

Mr. Andrew Lethbridge.

Dr. Joanna Mattingly of the Institute of Cornish Studies, Truro.

Cornish Studies Library of Redruth.

Courtney Library of the Royal Institute of Cornwall, Truro.

Mr. Alan (Mac) Lethbridge of Toowong, Australia.

Miss Megan Lethbridge of Tara, Queensland, Australia.

Mr. J. P. Derriman.

Mr. Gordon L. King for the portraits of Commander and Mrs. Phillip Parker King.

Mr. & Mrs. A. Dawe

Mr. Percy and Miss Marion Uglow

First published by Forget-Me-Not Books in 1999.

ISBN 1 870374 35 5

Copyright C. W. R. Winter 1999 ©. Photographs P. Winter 1999 ©.

Produced by Launceston Printing Company

Other published works by C. W. R. Winter include –

The Ancient Town of Yarmouth

The Manor House of the Isle of Wight.

Village Churches of the Isle of Wight (with photography by Pat Winter).

The 'Queen Mary': Her Early Years Recalled.

The Run of the Tide (with photography by Pat Winter and
        line drawings by Anthony Winter).

Travellers Joy (with photography by Pat Winter).

Long Live the Queen Mary.

The Enchanted Isle (with photography by Pat Winter).

Colourful Characters of the Isle of Wight.

Tales of the Isle of Wight.

Front Cover: The first view of the house as you come up the drive.

Back Cover: The 'round house', with Azaleas.

4

IN SUNDRY PLACES

Contents

Foreword

When the Winter family purchased Tregeare House in 1996 they could not have known that their lives would become immersed in the history of the previous occupants; their connections within the surrounding countryside, and 19th Century Australian settlers.

Ron Winter takes us on a captivating exploration of the countryside in and around the Hamlet of Tregeare, together with the historical involvement of the two Cornish families who form the principal "human element" of this book.

The families are those of Baron and Lethbridge, and throughout this book we follow them through successive generations, witnessing their successes and the trials that befell them during their 400 year association with Tregeare.

This beautifully illustrated book is an inspiring read for anybody interested in family history and the countryside. Furthermore it gives an illuminating insight into the late 19th Century social structure in and around Tregeare; similar of course to that of many communities throughout the land.

It has been profoundly satisfying to have been involved with this book, and I wish anybody who is encouraged through reading this book to research further into their home's history the best of luck!

Andrew Clive Baron Lethbridge

Preface

In offering this book to the public there are two things I must make clear. The first is that I feel a tremendous sense of privilege in being allowed to write it. To find somewhere as beautiful and peaceful as Tregeare and to have the opportunity of writing about it is enough to make anyone thankful, and humble.

And the second point follows naturally: In a world that is rapidly becoming electronic, push-button and noisy, and in which so many people seem to have forgotten about God, Tregeare is an oasis of peace. It is not unique, it is only a house, a woodland garden, and a few acres of agricultural land, and there are many other places as beautiful, but all those Barons and Lethbridges who have lived there have left something of their personalities behind and have contributed to the atmosphere. It is impossible to translate into words the beauty of the woodland garden, but to me it is convincing proof of a divine presence.

Many other people have contributed to the writing of this book and to its publication and it would have been nice to have mentioned them all by name. But as this is impossible I must just express a collective and sincere thank–you to them all and reserve a special mention to only a few. To Dorothy Lloyd who researched the Baron family, to David, Richard and (particularly) Andrew Lethbridge who have fed me with information about their illustrious family, and finally to members of my own family, to Rachael and Simon for their combined computer skills and hard work, to Pat for taking so many beautiful pictures and of course to Anthony who is doing such a splendid job at Tregeare and has already made the old house sit up and purr.

IN SUNDRY PLACES

Introduction

This is the story of a relatively small area of North Cornwall, an area of only a few square miles, situated just to the west of the River Tamar, which separates Cornwall from Devon, and not far from the original county town of Cornwall, Launceston.

The Castle on the Hill

For centuries the traveller from England into Cornwall had to pass right through Launceston, where the Norman castle, perched on top of its little hill, protecting its surrounding cottages, and looking for all the world like a mother hen sitting on her chicks, dominated the road. As a gateway into a strange and beautiful county it was, and still is, unsurpassed, though today the mighty dual carriageways of the A30 by-pass the town, thus saving it much distress. The castle is now an impressive ruin, but the town with its steep and narrow twisting streets has developed into as charming a place as one could imagine. True, there are modern shops and facilities, and business is bustling, but Launceston – pronounced *Lanson* by the locals – has not lost its medieval character nor its charm.

To the west of Launceston the traveller is in for a huge and pleasant surprise. The countryside is spread out in a patchwork of fields and woods, there are many hills and valleys, and several small crystal clear rivers such as the Kensey, the Ottery, the Amory, and the Inney. Other parts of England may boast a similar and equally beautiful countryside, but here there is something different, something intangible, something perhaps in the atmosphere. This is difficult to define, but nevertheless it is all pervading, all embracing, and very, very potent. Is it perhaps in the strange place names that greet you, the hundreds that start with Tre -, Pol -, or Pen -, the very large number named after Saints, who themselves have curious names? Can it possibly be something to do with the friendliness of the people you meet? Or the little country lanes, bounded by hedges on the top of banks, the carriageways innocent of white lines, and so narrow in places that travelling by motor car is an adventure?

There are many similarities in the Cornish countryside with that of Wales, and of course this is the principal reason why Cornwall is so different from England. It is a Celtic country, as is Wales, and the people of both lands have their roots deep in the past.

After the Roman occupation, England was invaded by Germans - Jutes, Angles and Saxons – large numbers of them all looking for somewhere to live. The German hunger for *lebensraum* is traditional and by no means a modern complaint, and it accounts for their periodic outbursts which have caused so much distress in Western Europe. When it happened in the 5th century A.D. the Celtic inhabitants in Britain were steadily pushed westwards into Wales and Cornwall, where they made their last stand.

There is no wonder then that there are similarities between the Cornish and the Welsh, no wonder that both are proud and stubborn, no wonder that they are traditionally suspicious of the English who so very long ago deprived them of their land. Both Cornwall and Wales are full of myths and legends and saints, they have both preserved their old native Celtic language, and incidentally they are both passionately addicted to singing, to male voice choirs, and to rugby football.

So the traveller from England, proceeding through Launceston to the West, is entering a new and strange county, and though it may be new to him it is in fact very, very old, a land in which legend and reality are inextricably mixed, where there is magic in the air, and where it is well to tread carefully, remembering the past. He will find legends by the score, many of them associated with King Arthur, the fabulous figure that poets have loved to write about and who is still very much alive today. King Arthur, with the help of Mallory and Tennyson, has spawned a thriving modern tourist industry in North Cornwall which provides the visitor with innumerable relics and souvenirs, and proudly shows him the lake in which King Arthur's sword, Excalibur, found its last resting place, not far from Slaughter Bridge where the great hero met his end.

In this land of myth and legend anything is possible. There are actually about a hundred towns, villages and localities known by the names of Celtic saints, many of whom originated in Wales, and indeed Welsh sounding names abound. The land is criss-crossed with ley lines or energy lines, call them what you will, and underneath a comparatively thin layer of topsoil there is granite, clay, and a wide, wide range of minerals. China clay is still mined in places, and Cornish tin has been world renowned since before the Christian era.

Tregeare Village Green

This then is the background against which the story of one particular small area is told. It lies mainly in the parish of Egloskerry, but spills over into the adjacent Laneast, and on the boundary between the two is the intriguing hamlet of Tregeare. Its history is by no means startling or world shaking, but it stretches back through many centuries and covers the varying fortunes of two large families. It takes us to sundry places in fact.

*The forbidding Keep
of Launceston Castle*

Our route lies Westward

The River Amory near Egloskerry

15

IN SUNDRY PLACES

Chapter 1 - Egloskerry

The village of Egloskerry lies four miles due west of Launceston, on a road that at one time was the main road to Camelford. Today the traffic on this road is comparatively light and the way is as leafy and as flower bedecked as one could wish for, as it passes through the village of St. Stephens, past Gallows Hill with its holy well, and skirting the golf course. To the south the views are occasionally stunning over miles and miles of beautiful countryside, and at one point a gap in the trees gives an equally breath-taking view to the north across the valley of the River Ottery, with the tower of North Petherwin church standing proud on the sky line.

Egloskerry village is small and self contained and consists of the church, the adjoining post office and stores, the primary school, and a cluster of houses. Its total population numbers around three hundred.

Egloskerry Church

The church is dedicated to St. Keria and gives the village its name, for "Eglos" is the Cornish name for a church, but in the 18th century for some reason an additional dedication to St. Petroc, a more widely known Cornish saint, was added. An extremely interesting history of the church, written by Barbara Leggatt, also suggests another possible Celtic dedication at one time to St. Ede or Eda.

It soon becomes apparent that both the church and village of Egloskerry are very old. St. Keria lived in the 5th century and is reputed to have searched for a suitable site between the rivers Ottery and Kensey on which to found an oratory. The site on which her church was founded is less than a mile from the Ottery, and only a quarter of a mile from the Kensey, and even nearer to the church is a well which has been attributed to her as a Holy Well. Until comparatively recently the waters of this well have been used to baptize village children, and no doubt it was once the principal source of water for the village.

But the site of the church is very much older than St. Keria. Those who believe in the significance of churchyard yew trees will say that the positioning of a single yew tree to the north of the church suggests that the site was used for pagan religious ceremonies in neolithic times, possibly as early as 1500 B.C. There is the remains of such a yew tree in Egloskerry churchyard to the north of the church, and as it was not an uncommon practice for Christians to build their churches on existing pagan sites, it is at least possible that Egloskerry has been a centre of habitation since before the Bronze Age.

The church as it stands today is basically Norman, but has lost much of its medieval and ancient character due to an extensive "restoration" in 1886 by the Victorians, who believed that to be holy a building had to be Gothic. The north wall of the nave however is Norman, as is the north transept and the north and east walls of the chancel, but much of the rest is 17th century with the exception of the tower which was added in the 15th century when church towers suddenly became fashionable.

Many churches built by the Normans were plain rectangular buildings, a design inherited from the Anglo-Saxons, and it is perhaps indicative of the importance of Egloskerry at that time that the church they built here originally was cruciform, which is a much more prestigious shape. Incidentally, the plain rectangular Anglo-Saxon design, roughly twice as long as it was wide and two stories high, with a steeply pitched roof, was a rather clever way of providing a basic building that could be used for one of three purposes, either as a house, or as a barn, or a church. And these three uses represent the basic and essential needs of human beings in this part of the world.

Houses are necessary as we have to have shelter, not being born with in-built fur coats like the animals. Barns are equally necessary as we have to have food, and basically this means either growing it or rearing it. And the third and most vital and essential need is that we all, every man, woman and child of us, must have some form of spiritual nourishment, and in the early days this was mainly provided by the church. The steeply pitched roof was necessary as all the best buildings at that time were thatched and a steep pitch was essential to encourage the rain to run off the thatch rather than soak through it.

In the north wall of the nave is a small door, now blocked up, popularly known as the Devil's Door, the superstition being that if Satan happened to get into the building a door in the nave gave him an exit and would prevent him getting into the chancel to do his evil work. On the outside of this doorway the tympanum is decorated with the carving of a fiery dragon, another device representing Satan, and this is believed to be the only one of its kind in Cornwall, although at one time there was a similar one in Tremaine church only a few miles away.

Though the present stone built church was erected almost exactly nine hundred years ago it is interesting to speculate about the previous modern wooden buildings on the site. The average life of a wooden building is in the region of two hundred years, so that the oratory established by St. Keria must have been replaced at least twice before the Normans decided to build in stone. Very little is known about St. Keria except that she was the daughter of St. Brychan after whom Brecon in Wales is named. He is said to have had twenty four children, which is not bad going for a saint, Keria being the eighteenth. Two of her sisters, Morwenna and Nona are also associated with this part of the West Country, Morwenna giving her name to Morwenstow and Nona to Altarnon, and St. Nona's well at Altarnon became celebrated in the middle ages when it became a place of pilgrimage to those seeking a cure to physical disabilities.

Records of the pre-Norman church in Egloskerry are inevitably scanty, and not until the stone building was in existence towards the end of the 11th century are any dates available which can be regarded as reliable. It would seem that in the early years of the 12th century the life of Egloskerry church was closely associated with two religious foundations in Launceston. The first of these was the Priory of St. Stephens–by–Launceston which was founded in 1067 but which suffered the fate of so many early Priories and was suppressed in 1120. In 1126 a new Priory was founded by Augustinian monks from Aldgate in London, and this one grew and thrived on a site alongside the River Kensey. It survived for over four hundred years, and by the beginning of the 16th century it was the wealthiest Priory in Cornwall, but alas in 1536 the avarice of King Henry V111 and the cupidity of his Chancellor, Thomas Cromwell, led to the Dissolution of the Monasteries, and the Priory-at-the-Ford was confiscated by the Crown.

The magnificent doorway at the White Hart Hotel

Little remains now of the beautiful range of buildings which were demolished at this time, and much of the stone would have been sold or otherwise acquired for building purposes. A good example of this practice can be seen in the magnificent stone doorway in the White Hart Hotel in Launceston which is reputed to have come from the Priory. All over England there was a mad scramble to acquire ex-monastery property after the Dissolution and there was a considerable change in ownership of land. Locally this applied to Egloskerry and its daughter Chapel-of-Ease at Tremaine, both of which belonged to the Priory and both of which now fell into the hands of local landowners.

Through all this period of great ecclesiastical upheaval Egloskerry and its ancient church managed to survive, though records of activity continue to be few and far between. No longer would monks from Launceston's Priory-at-the-Ford travel to the village to celebrate Mass, but services went on as they had done for the past several hundred years.

Looking back through the years one significant date has survived – September 14th in the year 1260 – nearly two hundred years after the building of the Norman church. On this date it is recorded that Bishop Branscombe dedicated an altar either in or from the Chapel of Tregeare, but there is no supporting evidence of this. The story is repeated by more than one writer, and it is not clear whether the altar had come from the Chapel of Tregeare and was being dedicated in Egloskerry church, or whether the ceremony was being held in the Tregeare Chapel. If the latter then the question arises as to whether the Tregeare mentioned is the one only two miles from Egloskerry, or whether it refers to an entirely different Tregeare in the parish of St. Gerrans. The consensus of opinion would appear to be in favour of the local Tregeare which is actually within the parish of Egloskerry, but at this distance in time it is hardly a matter of vital importance.

Next door to the church is the village Post Office and Stores, an attractive white painted old building. Before it became a post office it served as the village inn and it is not difficult to imagine it in this role. The shop has a massive stone floor that would grace any country village pub, but the interesting thing about this inn is that it was known as the Simcoe Arms, named after the Rev. H.A. Simcoe.

Mr Simcoe was not only the vicar but also Lord of the Manor and hence a figure of some importance in the district. Besides owning property in Devonshire he bought the local manor of Penheale in 1830 which covered the whole of Egloskerry Parish and much of the Parish of Tremaine. Ownership of the manor also gave him the Advowson of the Church, that is, the right to appoint the Vicar, and who better to choose than himself, though he did not become Vicar until 1846. Who christened the village inn is not known, but as the Simcoe Arms it gave him a foot in both camps as it were, and somehow this seems quite appropriate.

Mr Simcoe was obviously a man of parts, for he also achieved local fame as a writer and printer, establishing the Penheale Press in order to publish a series of books he wrote entitled "Light from the West." He was also socially well connected with one of the leading families in the area, the Lethbridges of Tregeare, one of his daughters Elizabeth Lethbridge Simcoe marrying a Colonel Willoughby Trevelyan in 1859. This marriage was witnessed by several members of the Lethbridge family, as was the wedding in 1847 of another of his daughters, Anne Eliza Simcoe, to Sedley Basterd Marke Esquire of Plymouth who round about this time purchased the old farm and house of Treludick in Egloskerry. Lake's History of Cornwall mentions that after Mr Marke's death his widow remained one of the principal landowners in the area, together with the Rev. H.A. Simcoe and J.C.B. Lethbridge Esq.

IN SUNDRY PLACES

Chapter 2 - The Road to Tregeare

In the centre of Egloskerry village, as you turn into the Piper's Pool road, you cannot help but notice the beech tree. This is an enormous and beautiful plant standing on a grassy mound to the right and under it are one or two shrubs, a seat, and the village notice board. This latter is an important part of village life for on it are notices of practically everything that is happening in the village. Typical of the information that can be obtained here is the date of the next meeting of the Parish Council or of a talk in the Village Hall organised by the Gardening Club, a list of all the Services being held in the Parish Church during the current month, or the opening to the public of the gardens at Penheale Manor. All the important facts in fact.

For this is the centre of village communications, a glimpse into the structure of community life, together with an invitation to join in and become part of that community, a chance to meet the local people who are the life blood of the village. In most of the notices the invitation is mute and somewhat impersonal, but occasionally one gives a closer look into the life of the place, as for example, the carefully written notice saying that a sixteen year old boy is available for gardening, pond clearing, or dog walking, etc. How many ponds, one wonders, did he manage to clear through this advertisement?

Egloskerry is not alone in having a communications centre; every village has one in some form or another, and vital they are to community life. There are other vital contributions too, as witness the flower bed just across the road from the notice board. This is only a small bed, and it is outside the gate leading to the back of two cottages, but it is always full of colour and is a joy as one walks down the road. In the spring and summer it is full of flowers, and even at the back end of the year, when all gardens are beginning to look a trifle bedraggled, it still manages to catch the eye and strike a cheerful note. Whoever tends this little flower bed does not shout about it or advertise the fact in any way, but it is a valuable and positive contribution to the life of the village, and one that is much appreciated

The Piper's Pool road, as it leaves the centre of the village, executes a decided S – bend and even the most frenetic motorist has to slow down and take it with care. On foot, and when there are no cars or aircraft about, there is a strange feeling of peace as one walks through the middle of the S. Now, whether this is due to the fact that the twists in the road provide an insulation from the world on either hand, or whether it is due to something in the atmosphere of the place it is impossible to say. But at this point the road passes between a very old and almost derelict shippon on the left hand side, and a grassy bank with many wild flowers on the other, and the feeling of tranquillity descends.

Once past this grassy bank the entrance to Skinnish Farm opens out, and then by the roadside is the Village Hall. On the left hand side of the road are the entrances to several gardens, in one of which at least is a profusion of that strange plant, the Indian Balsam, which has the curious habit of ejecting its seeds with explosive force in order to ensure as wide a distribution as possible. Some of the seeds have indeed reached the roadside, for this tall and beautiful plant with its pink flowers can be seen growing in the hedgerows here in late summer.

The entrance to Well Meadow on the left suggests that this is the way to the Holy Well, but alas this is not so for this little road is a dead end and leads only to a small housing estate of fifteen modern bungalows, and to reach the well one has to approach from the other side of the meadow opposite the Church. where there is a public footpath. Sadly the well was forgotten and ignored for many many years but was rescued from oblivion by the bungalow dwellers on whose back garden it abuts. They cleared away the brambles and nettles that were choking it, and have since encouraged wild flowers to grow in the little well enclosure so that it can at least now be seen. The little structure erected over the source of the spring is rather crude and dilapidated, having seen better days, and a face-lift is long overdue. The history of this well, which goes back at least to the time of St. Keria in the 6th century surely merits a little thought on this subject.

Past Well Meadow the lane dips downhill between high hedges, and when it levels off and swings to the left it crosses what was once the railway line at Egloskerry Station. The line can be traced on the map through many miles of the most beautiful scenery on its way to the coast, and once connected this part of North Cornwall to civilisation. Today only a couple of miles or so still remains, of narrow gauge track running from Launceston, and many people regret the loss of this facility which would without doubt have proved a great tourist attraction in this day and age.

Egloskerry Station House is now a private dwelling but the old platform still remains together with its large sign, and the owner has imported a railway carriage as a reminder of the past. Where the track once crossed the lane the County Council have painted a huge 30 in an oval cartouche on the road as a warning to motorists entering the village, giving the impression of being a gigantic hopscotch marking, or alternatively a mini helicopter landing sign.

Only a few yards further on the lane crosses the River Kensey and a seat has been provided on the bank so that a weary traveller may sit and rest in the peace and quiet of the countryside and listen to the gurgling of the water in the stream. The Kensey is a small but delightful river and in summer it does not carry a great amount of water, but this is normally crystal clear and weed free. After rain it can rise rapidly and become muddy as the water drains off the land, and it is not unknown for the river to flood the road in protracted wet spells. Parallel to the Kensey and only a few hundred yards further on is another small river, the Amory, and these two streams meet together in the fields below the village and continue on their joint way to Launceston and beyond. In Launceston the river passes the site of the Priory-at-the-Ford before joining the larger River Tamar which for many miles provides the boundary between Cornwall and Devon.

The road leads uphill to Badharlick and Tregeare

The road to Tregeare hives off to the right between the two rivers and begins to climb uphill to Badharlick. Within a couple of hundred yards is Badharlick Mill and next to it the Miller's House, and at first sight this is a curious position for a water mill as it is midway between two rivers and must be at least six feet above their level. Nevertheless it had at one time its own water supply and was a large and thriving mill, driving three pairs of stones. From the 11th century onwards it was obligatory to grind corn at the mill belonging to the Lord of the Manor, and Badharlick Mill owed its popularity to the local manor of Penheale.

The element *Bad-* in the name Badharlick implies the presence of a spring or some source of water, and there are a number of place names in this county that demonstrate this. But the word is more popular in Germany where *Bad* can literally mean *a bath*, and in the Rhine Valley there are several towns and villages which owe their name to the presence of water, such as Bad Kreuznach, Bad Durkheim and Wiesbaden, culminating in Baden Baden, a town famous in Edwardian days for its curative waters.

A little higher up the lane from the Mill is the hamlet of Badharlick itself, small, self contained, and consisting of two farms, a few cottages and little else, but nevertheless a bustling and thriving community which has been active in the agricultural history of the neighbourhood for several centuries. It is the little hamlets like Badharlick which are the core and heart of rural Britain, giving the countryside its unique flavour, and producing a never - ending stream of country folk who are truly the back bone of the nation. There will be more to be said about Badharlick later in our story, but at the moment we are climbing the hill on our way to Tregeare where other interests await us.

Since we left the level of the Kensey and Amory rivers the lane has climbed steadily, and when it finally levels off the Ordnance Survey maps quote a figure of 175 metres above sea level. At this point the

Triangulation Point high on Tregeare Down

higher hedges which have enclosed the lane disappear and there is a great feeling of coming out into the open. To the left the ground falls away and though there is more high ground on the right the sensation of being near the top of a hill persists. The lane enters a green tunnel between the trees and in a countryside that is full of beautiful lanes this must be one of the most beautiful. This is Tregeare Down, the highest point of which at 219 metres is marked on the map with a Triangulation Point and the name Tregearedown Beacon. The lane skirts the top of the hill and then with a sudden dip and swing to the left enters a short avenue of ancient oaks, under which is a sign telling us that we have arrived at our immediate destination – Tregeare. This unassuming little hamlet is the very epicentre of our story.

The road to the West

Centre of Egloskerry Village

The road leading to Tregeare

Village post box

IN SUNDRY PLACES

Chapter 3 - Tregeare

The little hamlet of Tregeare rightly starts down in the dip where the road swings in from Egloskerry and the avenue of oak trees begins. At this point another lane joins the road from the left, this being South Drive, originally planned by the owner of the Tregeare Estate many years ago when he was one of the most important landowners in North Cornwall and wished the world to recognise this fact. At the other end of this Drive, in Pipers Pool, was his South Lodge, a full mile and a half away which he must have felt was an indication of his importance.

The avenue of oaks has suffered over the years but still makes an interesting and intriguing approach to the few buildings that comprise the hamlet. Firstly on the left is Home Farm with a pleasant stone farmhouse and a cluster of farm buildings. Outside the house on wash days a line of washing is silhouetted against the sky, a homely and friendly touch. Opposite, on the right hand side of the road is the slightly leaning end of a derelict barn containing the remains of a once smart window, and also a bright red post box, a further indication that life still goes on.

Here the lane opens out to show a small village green and on the left more stone barns, now partially hidden by trees. Several of these barns have already been converted, quite skilfully, into desirable residences, and this complex is known as Baron Court, the Baron family having once owned Tregeare and much of the surrounding land. Ahead lies the entrance to Tregeare House down a long winding drive through the trees, the house itself being invisible from the road at this point. On the left of the gateway is The Lodge, once known as North Lodge, this being a veritable Hansel and Gretel type cottage, built in 1866.

On reaching the village green it is advisable to pause for a moment, for two reasons. The first is that this is the centre of this small hamlet, and the second is simply to drink in the peace and tranquillity of the place, which here is in abundance, and which in this busy modern world is a much needed tonic, and one which is completely free to anyone who will pause, relax, and give thanks. In fact, you just listen to the silence and it does you good.

Front Gate
Tregeare House

It must immediately be added that this silence can be, and is occasionally, shattered by the passing overhead of a low flying aircraft, but this does not happen very often. When it does it is well to remember that nearly sixty years ago the free world was saved for us by a bunch of intrepid young men who flew the lethal aircraft of their day and in 1940 won the Battle of Britain for us. Until men have learnt to settle their differences by talking instead of fighting it behoves us to be grateful to these young fliers of today who streak across the skies at ever increasing speeds and in their passing inadvertently frighten us and the animals that we tend.

Another and less devastating noise can occasionally be heard in Tregeare from the farmer's tractor as it goes about its business, and this is well worth noting. In the old days cows were usually taken out to graze, and brought back for milking, by a man or a boy and a dog, and though these two are still necessary the man now rides behind in his tractor, the dog and the cows between them doing all the necessary work of navigation. Presumably if only the dog could be taught how to open and close gates the farmer would not have to attend at all.

Before leaving Tregeare Green note the only other building in sight, this being Greystones a Victorian house on the right, built in 1879. In the cluster of buildings near Baron Court is one that was originally the village Post Office, now a private house, and tucked out of sight beyond Greystones is Tregeare Methodist Chapel, sadly no longer in constant use. Cornwall is of course famous for its chapels, Methodism being very vigorous in the Duchy, and for the same reason there are very few public houses about, since alcoholic drink and Methodism do not normally mix.

Greystones across the Green

The road through the centre of Tregeare continues on towards Camelford, and only a few hundred yards from the Green is the parish boundary between Egloskerry and Laneast, a granite post in the hedge marking the spot where it crosses the road. Tregeare House, a Palladian mansion built in 1790 by Jasper Baron is just inside Laneast parish, and the back of the house and stable block can be seen quite close to the road.

This is really all there is to Tregeare, a country road, a few old stone barns and cottages – and Tregeare House which has dominated the area for the last two hundred years. But there is of course more to it than that; there is something else that gives life and character to all these buildings and inanimate objects, and this is the human element, all the people, hundreds and hundreds of them who over the centuries have lived here, worked here, tilled the land and planted crops. People who have lived through good times and bad times, years when the weather has turned sour and the crops have failed, years when the sun has shone at the right time and their harvest festival has been a true thanksgiving.

Unfortunately we know very little about these people of past ages and their individual lives, for the majority of residents leave no records behind them. A few who achieve local prominence are remembered on the walls of churches and on headstones, but even these records only go back a few hundred years, and time and weather make their messages more and more difficult to read. But for most people there is little to go on and we are groping in the dark, trying to piece together scraps of inadequate information in an attempt to recreate their character. And as we probe further back in time, so the information becomes fainter, dimmer and less reliable, so that the odds on being able to find out how people loved or hated, or dealt with life's other problems such as sickness and tragedy, become longer and longer.

When human life first began in this part of North Cornwall men were hunters, a nomadic people living on the animals or fish they could catch together with nuts and berries, and it was many hundreds of years before groups began to settle down and build permanent homes, tilling the land and growing or rearing the food they ate. The single yew tree in Egloskerry churchyard to the north of the church suggests that people were settled there in neolithic times and had adopted the site as being sacred, but this could be a wild exaggeration.

Another indication of activity in times almost as remote is the earthwork and beacon site on the top of Tregeare Down. At first sight this too looks very old and it is easy to be led astray by romantic notions of wild men dressed in skins uttering strange cries and fighting for their lives, or engaged in some lurid mystical ceremony. But the truth is probably much more prosaic.

The earthwork consists of an enclosure measuring approximately one hundred and fifty feet (forty six metres) by one hundred and twenty feet (thirty six metres) and surrounding it there is an intermittent bank and ditch. At one time archaeologists thought this was of neolithic origin and had been a camp, but experience told them it was really too small and it was unlikely to have been older than the Iron Age, or even later Roman times. This theory too had to be abandoned, and was then replaced by the possibility of its being a beacon site of medieval date or even later, there being insufficient evidence of any earlier use.

The idea of a beacon blazing away on the top of the hill is exciting, and immediately one thinks of the Spanish Armada, and of Sir Francis Drake and his brave boys awaiting its arrival in Plymouth only a few miles away, but unfortunately a dampener was put on this possibility by the Ordnance Survey who pointed out that the earthwork was slightly below the top of the hill and would therefore have had restricted views to the north east, which was one of the directions in which a warning beacon would need to be seen. The Ordnance Survey claimed modestly that their own triangulation point on the hilltop only a few metres away would have been a much better spot for a beacon.

The final theory as to the origin of the earthwork was matter-of-fact and practical. Noting that within the retaining bank the earth appeared to have been hollowed out, and that the centre is waterlogged, it was suggested that it had originally been constructed as a pond and that it was no older than the 17th or 16th centuries. And with this theory we have to be content, comforted by the fact that the site is at least several hundreds of years old and is unspoilt, and that the Down does shelter the little hamlet of Tregeare from any north-easterly weather.

IN SUNDRY PLACES

Chapter 4 - Tregeare House

When the Tregeare Estate was put on the market in the mid 1990's the Agent described the house in the following terms.

"Tregeare House is a Grade II listed building, constructed mainly of rendered stone and slate roofing. The house separates into three distinct parts, the elegant main residence, a self contained wing and a further wing currently arranged as offices. To the north east of the house is a listed stone stable block with garaging, a useful range of out-buildings, and a listed Lodge Cottage. The gardens have some of the earliest (and now largest) Rhododendrons in England as well as many fine specimens of Camellia, Azalea, Magnolia and Euchryphia. The main house enjoys fine views across its own parkland towards a lake which was constructed originally as a fresh water swimming pool. In all there is about 85 acres of woodland providing good rough shooting."

Tregeare House from the Park

Estate Agents are normally prone to exaggeration, but this one was modest to a degree. To describe the house as 'elegant' is to do it less than justice, and to risk damning it with faint praise, for all too often this sort of label is attached to buildings of little architectural merit, or those in a scruffy condition with a multitude of deficiencies to hide.

But the sight of the house, as one proceeds up the drive, arouses several different emotions, the first one probably being surprise, for what is a Palladian style building doing amid all these leafy Cornish lanes? This is clearly something different. Elegance there certainly is in abundance, and the house sits comfortably in its park-like surroundings with no hint of incongruity, but it is indubitably intriguing that a building of this type should be there at all. Actually, to anyone interested in architecture the best view of the house is from the south west, for it is from this point that the full beauty of the west front, with its perfect proportions and classical pediment, can be seen.

And it is this west front, a superb example of Palladian architecture, that Jasper Baron first built in 1790, and the fact that he was only twenty two years old at the time adds to the intrigue. Whatever possessed a young Cornishman, descended from a long line of farmers, to build such a grandiloquent Italianate 18th century house amid his Cornish fields? At the time, towards the end of the 18th century, there was a strong Italianate influence in English architecture, largely because it had become fashionable for the sons of rich fathers to be sent on the Grand Tour of Europe to complete their education. Inevitably these young men came back full of ideas on how to spend their father's money, and building something new and exciting was often at the head of the list.

Whether Jasper Baron did or did not do the Grand Tour is immaterial but he certainly did follow the fashion of the age and build a most remarkable house, one that has excited comment ever since. Another question immediately comes to mind: where did the money come from to build this mansion? For this is not the sort of house to be built out of proceeds of even a very successful farm business, this house is definitely a gentleman's residence, requiring considerable capital outlay and a sustainable income for its maintenance.

The answer to this question is simple though romantic, and in a later chapter, when we consider in more detail the Baron family, much will be revealed. But at present let it suffice that the money was originally generated in the City of London in mid 18th century by Jasper's Great-great-uncle George who made a fortune there as a merchant. George died in 1686 and left a large sum of money in Trust to his family for the sole purpose of "buying estates of inheritance." Why this fund was allowed to lie fallow for three generations it is difficult to say, but it must have grown during this period, and perhaps it needed the initiative of a young man to get things on the move. Jasper's father Oliver died in 1786 when Jasper was eighteen years old and though he was not the first-born son it was he who persuaded the Trustees to let him have the money.

The story goes that there was previously a farmhouse on this site, and that as it possessed a better view than any other house on his estates it was chosen by Jasper as the site for his new mansion. On to this old farmhouse he superimposed the magnificent West front, but he was never destined to go much further than this as he died in 1798 at the age of thirty. Jasper Baron left a widow, Elizabeth, a son William aged one year, and an as yet unborn daughter Elizabeth Ann, and it was Mrs Baron who during the next twenty years not only brought up her family but also completed the building of the house.

The South front became the main front and is symmetrical about a central portico with Ionic columns, the porch being capped by a classical cornice. The house has two stories topped by a heavily modillioned cornice, which gives it a severely classical appearance, and behind this is a slate hipped roof. There is an attic storey which originally contained three large bedrooms but which was altered during one of the several stages of alteration carried out in the 19th and 20th centuries. Other alterations to the original building included the adding on of the service wings to right and left in the 19th century. But from the front the house looks very much as it must have been nearly two hundred years ago when Elizabeth Baron completed it. She must have obtained great satisfaction from her work, and have felt that Jasper would have approved.

Looking from the front of the house across the broad sweeping lawn to the south the view is extensive, with Bodmin Moor in the distance. On either side of the lawn are rhododendrons, some of the earliest, and by now the largest, imported into England from the Black Sea area. Their size and beauty are outstanding, they are now much higher that the house itself, and in Spring are a mass of bloom, for all the world like giant pin cushions of colour. They make a perfect setting for this dazzling white Palladian House, and together with the Camellias, Azaleas, Magnolias and Euchryphias which abound are a spectacular feature of Tregeare.

A Rhododedron higher than the house

At ground floor level the inside layout of the house is conventional. Entering through the double front door into the hall there are doors on either side into the large principal reception rooms, the one on the left being the Library, from which through double doors is the large dining room. At the back of the hall is an archway leading to the staircase hall, the stair-case being impressive and of cantilever design. At the end of the staircase hall is a green baize covered door into the domestic quarters of the house with access to both wings, the east wing being a self-contained three bedroom staff house. Just inside the door is a long row of staff bells connecting to all the principal rooms of the house, and here too is the old kitchen, the only easily recognisable remains of the farmhouse that occupied this site in the years before 1790. Other reminders of the old farmhouse can be seen in various walls in the rear part of the house.

The staircase well is lighted by a long and slender window of stained glass, and this bears an inscription in Latin to confirm that the house was indeed built by Jasper Baron in 1790. This window also carries two armorial shields, one of the Lethbridge family who inherited Tregeare by marriage from the Barons, and the other representing the Barons themselves. At the top of the stairs at first floor level is a splendid galleried landing which has a screen of fluted Ionic columns, the turned balusters lining the stairs being continued right round the landing in a most satisfying manner.

There are five principal bedrooms, four dressing rooms and several bathrooms in the main part of the house, but towards the rear, owing to the several major alterations that have occurred during the last two hundred years, the layout of rooms is unconventional and a small self-contained flat has been incorporated which together with the west wing provides additional accommodation and an excellent study and offices. Traces of the old farmhouse walls can be seen in this rear part of the house, together with two small staircases. On the second and attic floor the three original bedrooms have been combined into one large apartment, used as a playroom.

One of the joys of Tregeare House is in the quality of the materials used in its construction, and in the high standard of workmanship employed, not only in its building but also in its alterations and maintenance. All the principal doors, both up and down stairs are six panelled and are of very solid construction, with panelled reveals and pediments to the doorcases leading from the hall to the rooms on left and right. The door furniture is of equally good quality.

The pre-1790 kitchen

All the principal windows are twelve pane sashes though old pictures of the house show that in the late 19th century some of these had been replaced with larger panes, resulting in a considerable loss of elegance. Fortunately a recent restoration has returned these to their original true beauty.

Another feature of the principal rooms is the wealth of moulded plaster cornices and central roses, those in the library and dining room having survived from the original part of the house built by Jasper Baron. These are of very high quality, as indeed are all the mouldings whether of plaster or of wood. The wooden architrave mouldings, dado rails and skirting boards are intricate in design and equally satisfying.

The Lodge and Village Green

Bringing the cows in for milking

View to the south

Tregeare House from the south-west

During its lifetime the house has experienced varying fortunes and at one time in the early 1980's, after having been a family residence for over one hundred and fifty years, it was for a period empty and forlorn. During this spell it was visited by the Cornish historian and poet, A.L.Rowse who wrote the following mournful lines about it –

Tregeare

Tregeare – how lonely stands the gaunt house,
Lonely and unloved, indeed deserted,
The last member of the former family gone.
The house stands tall and shuttered,
Blind windows that were once open
To look across the level spaces of lawn
To distant Bodmin Moor on summer horizon.
Once the meet would be here on dewy mornings,
Red coats gay on their mounts, sleek horses,
The hounds impatient to be gone over moor
And field and stream. The family would come
Out on the terrace, stand on the columned porch
Dispensing hospitality, that became impossible:
Farms sold one by one, things folding up,
Life slowing down. Where, in days gone by,
In lush Victorian days, sons home from India,
Under grandparents' rule, the old squire and wife,
Not a weed would show in the forecourt,
Where the stable clock stands at twenty to three,
As it has stood for twenty years. Dorothy's
Thatched summer house, where she played
Games as a girl, now falling in together,
Her garden she cared for to the end
Overgrown, weeds, honeysuckle, columbine,
A pathetic rusty watering-can on its side.
Peer down the walks, the unkempt drive,
Rhododendron and camellia interlaced
With strangling brambles, nettles, bindweed.
And yet, O once, in early May the mountain
Of purple ponticum would put forth its glory:
The cedar summon the shades to tea in its shadow,

A footman to bring it, chatelaine in bombazine
To preside over friendly group at table –
Where today all is emptiness and vacancy.
The gate clangs behind the trespasser
Upon all this shuttered vanished life, and still
Stands the stable clock at twenty to three.

A.L.Rowse

At this time Tregeare's fortunes had reached a very low ebb, but in September 1982 the House and its now much reduced estate was sold by auction, and during the next fourteen years the new owner did much to revive it and bring it back to life. Once again though Fate decreed that a change of ownership was necessary, and this took place in July 1996. With this change new hope came to Tregeare, spirits rose, and the subsequent basic and caring restoration that was immediately begun has already transformed, not only the house itself, but also the eighty five acres of wooded grounds and the remainder of the estate, and it is already no exaggeration to say that in its two hundred year history the house and estate have never looked, and been, in better condition than they are at present. And the future indeed looks bright.

Dining Room

The Library

*Pedimented door from
Hall to Library*

*Galleried landing with
fluted ionic columns*

IN SUNDRY PLACES

Chapter 5 - The Baron Family

The story of the restoration of Tregeare must begin with the Baron family who created it in its present form, and this takes us back several hundred years. The Baron name, in its various spellings, is well known in the West Country, and over the centuries the family tree has acquired many branches, the main stem being inevitably connected with farming. Intermarriage with similar farming families has complicated the issue, and a general expansion in several other directions has also caused the 'canopy' of the tree to spread far beyond the boundaries of Devon and Cornwall.

Before the establishment of Parish Registers in the early 16th century records are unreliable, and the rise and fall of these little farming empires is not always easy to follow. The particular one in which we are interested is mainly concentrated in the parishes of Egloskerry and Laneast, but with off shoots in Stratton, Marhamchurch, Tintagel and Mevagissey among others. In sundry places in fact.

Barons were settled in these parishes possibly as early as the 13th or 14th centuries, and in tracing them back into these dim and distant times there is immediately an additional problem, which is that of spelling the name. Obviously one has to accept that the name could be spelled either with one 'R' or two, but to find it spelled BARNE or BARNES is perhaps a surprise. But it has to be remembered that hundreds of years ago very few people could read or write, especially in country districts, and that the parish clerk himself, who was responsible for keeping the registers, was probably not over educated and would be taking down names phonetically. So that the name that went into the book would be what it sounded like to the clerk, and if the man who was giving his name did not speak clearly, or had a very strong accent, then almost anything might happen. With a Cornish accent there is very little difference between Baron and Barne.

Some of the names, and other words, recorded in 16th and 17th century parish documents are really quite comical to us now, and though they make the researcher's task more difficult they do also make it much more interesting. A typical example that springs to mind is from an Egloskerry Parish lease dated October 1614 in which it is stipulated that the rent of two shillings (if demanded) shall be paid "on some Sondaie immediately after the end of morning prayer" and it goes on to mention "the hireing of six of the beste and substanchialst men of the said p'ishe.'

Another complication with the Barons of Egloskerry is that so many of them are called John and it is easily possible to get them mixed. When there are two John Barons around at the same time one of them is often referred to as 'John Baron the Elder' and the other as 'the Younger', but what happens when the elder one dies? It is not uncommon to find a John Baron referred to at different times by several alternative patronyms, and it is true that the path of this type of research is fraught with numerous pitfalls. Perhaps the only safe way is to describe him as being of a particular place, but even this is treacherous, for as a young bachelor he will probably continue to live with his parents, and not until he marries will he move into a farm of his own.

Badharlick Mill, once the official Mill of the Manor

Which brings us to a particular John Baron of Badharlick who is one of the first of whom we have a record. Perhaps you will remember Badharlick, the little farming community in the parish of Egloskerry lying halfway between Egloskerry village and Tregeare, and where beside a couple of farms there is a water mill belonging to the Lord of the Manor of Penheale. Indeed, in the Middle Ages the water mill helped to make Badharlick quite an important little place since all corn grown in the Manor had to be ground there. At its busiest the mill was driving three pairs of stones which is not bad going for a small country mill.

John Baron had several children and it would seem that there were two boys, both of whom were called John. This may sound highly improbable but in this generation there are records of a John Baron the elder and a John Baron the Younger.

Badharlick

One of these married an Alice Rogers and their names appear in a Manor Court Roll dated November 1566 which at least enables us to establish a time scale. This John Baron died in 1619 but it is his brother who died in 1624 who interests us more since he is buried in Egloskerry Church and we have a copy of his Will which gives us a glimpse, if somewhat confusing, into his family affairs.

Incidentally, these two John Barons had a sister Elizabeth who married an Andrew Congden. Andrew died and she re-married a William Basterd, but in the interim while she was a widow she got into trouble with the Manor Court, on 3rd December 1577, through failing to send her corn to the Lord of the Manor's mill to be ground. This manorial privilege of grinding every farmer's corn was a regular source of income to the manor and was jealously guarded.

46

At this point tribute must be paid to two people, a brother and sister, who in the 1960's were so intrigued with their own relationship to the Baron family that they researched its origins in some depth, and produced a mass of information stretching back to the Norman occupation in the 11th century. Major Oliver Baron Shoubridge and his sister Mrs Evaline Dorothy Lloyd between them unearthed information about nearly 200 members of the Baron family, and their descent from the Barons of Egloskerry via the Rev. John Baron who died in Pattishall, Northamptonshire in 1763.

Many of the male descendants of Rev. John Baron were given the additional Christian name of Baron, and this has preserved the name, and as will be seen later on another family, that of Lethbridge, has achieved the same result. Considering that Major Shoubridge did not live in Cornwall, and that Mrs Lloyd together with her husband was running a busy farm, the amount of information they unearthed was phenomenal. They did not manage to dot every 'i' nor cross every 't', but their patient and painstaking work, and Mrs Lloyd's written record of it, has earned the gratitude of all other researchers who have thus been saved hours of initial investigation.

So John Baron of Badharlick died in 1624 and was buried in Egloskerry Church. His grave lies in the South Porch and the slate stone carries the following inscription.

"Here lyeth the body of John Barne of Badhallocke
who departed this life November in the year of our Lord 1624."

"As 'tis uncertain when death's stroke shall fall
Tis certain once that it will light on all
Here hee doth sleep whose vertuous life on earth
Did shine till death did stopp his vitall breath
Hee clothed the naked nere did shutt his door
Against the indigent or hungry poore
Yet deedes of pitty reach not to his love
He iniur'd none his heart was fixt above
But though his corps with worms be turned to mould
His soul with angels doth God's face behold
When not a barne on earth earth's corn shall hide
This barne in heaven shall be deifiede
A glorious temple ever to remaine
And there enjoy ye never failing graine."

John Baron must have been quite a character to have merited such an effusion on his gravestone, the majority of us have to be content with the bare statement of the facts, or at best a message of the "gone but not forgotten" variety.

His will contains over 20 legacies to various people, many of them children of his brothers and sisters, for example he leaves £10 "to the children of Andrew Congden, deceased," and £10 "to Grace, the daughter of Elizabeth Basterd, my sister," which tells us that Elizabeth was widowed at a fairly early age and was still young enough to have at least one child from her second marriage.

John Baron also owned various bits of property in the area and left three houses to his nephew George who was the son of his deceased elder brother John. One of these was in Tregeare and the other two in Badgall the little hamlet only a mile or so from Tregeare along the Camelford Road. He had other property in the parish of Altarnon, at Trecollas and Trerithick, that he left to a William Basterd who was possibly the husband of his sister Elizabeth.

His principal bequest of property was to his widow, another Elizabeth. He had married her only ten years previously as his second wife, and there were no children of the marriage. His first wife had given him a son and a daughter but both had died in infancy. So John Baron had no direct descendants, which explains why his property was distributed amongst his remaining closest relations. A further, and substantial, bequest was made to another son of his elder brother, this nephew being described later as John Baron of Treludick.

This is the first mention of Treludick as a property of the Baron family, and it turned out to be a very important one. If it is true, and it would certainly seem to be, that there is a turning point in the fortunes of every family, it was at this time that the Barons of Egloskerry began to blossom and bear fruit. They had been doing very nicely thank you up to this point, but with the acquisition of Treludick events began to speed up and the family fortunes took on a different complexion. It is purely a coincidence that it was at about this time too that William Shakespeare wrote his tragedy of Julius Caesar in which he states –

"There is a tide in the affairs of men,
Which, taken at the flood, leads on to fortune;
Omitted, all the voyage of their life
Is bound in shallows and miseries."

IN SUNDRY PLACES

Chapter 6 - Treludick

The farmstead of Treludick is situated about one and a half miles to the west of the village of Egloskerry. It lies a few hundred yards north of the highway in an area of great beauty and tranquility and has obviously been there for many a long year. On Ordnance Survey Maps the name is printed in a gothic type-face as an indication that it is a site considerable antiquity. A study of the local map provides some interesting examples of other buildings shown in this old fashioned way, Launceston Castle of course, Penheale Manor, which was established before the Norman Conquest, the earthwork on Tregearedown and several Tumuli. Cornwall is particularly rich in reminders of its historical past, and printing these names in a different way is an effective method of nudging us into remembering this fact. So the maps frequently print words such as 'Cross' or 'Holy Well,' and some other names that perhaps one would not expect such as 'Trerithick Bridge' and at a nearby fork in the highway 'Guide Post.'

Treludick's front garden

Treludick got its name from a family that owned it in the 12th century and lived there for several hundred years, until the time came when they ran out of male heirs and it passed out of their ownership through marriage. It came into the possession of the Sleeman family, and under them continued to prosper.

On 3rd August 1607 Joan Sleeman, only daughter of George Sleeman, Yeoman, married John Baron the nephew of the John Baron of Badharlick who died in 1624. Young John was twenty six years old, having been born in November 1581, and his bride must have been even younger, and though their marriage only lasted twenty two years – Joan died in 1639 – in that period she gave birth to eleven children. Indeed, it could well be that child bearing wore her out and was the ultimate cause of her death, for of her eleven children three died in childhood and one other lived only to the age of thirty.

Rear of house, protected by rising ground from the prevailing weather

With hindsight, we have the knowledge that within the next five generations there were seven more early deaths, and that by 1833 this particular line of the Barons had ceased to exist. Infant mortality at this time was notoriously high, and there were periodic outbursts of infectious diseases, all loosely described as 'the plague' and brought about mainly by the lack of sanitation, that killed both young and old, and also of course life expectancy was considerably lower than today, fifty years being regarded as a good ripe old age. But so many early deaths must prompt the question as to whether there might be some genetic disorder somewhere along the line.

Our particular interest in John and Joan Baron and their children stems from the fact that it is from them that we first begin to see the descent through these next five generations to Jasper Baron who built the present Tregeare House in 1790. The family tree showing this is given on page 52.

In September 1620 George Sleeman, Joan's father, made an indenture with John to establish the ownership of his considerable properties in the area. John and Joan had been married for thirteen years and already had five children, Mary who was born in 1609, John their eldest son born 1611, Elizeus born 1613, Elizabeth born 1615 and Degory born 1618. Joan was once again pregnant and their sixth child Katherine was born in the following March. They were all, including George Sleeman himself, already living at Treludick, or were on the point of living there.

The last proviso is necessary since the indenture states that Treludick is at present in the possession of one Tristram Martin, but it goes on to say that from henceforth Treludick together with five other properties in the parishes of Laneast, Davidstow, St. Clether and Altarnon shall belong unconditionally to George Sleeman for the term of his natural life, and then after his death to "the said John Baron the younger and the said Johan his wife and the issues of their bodies lawfully begotten and to the begotten."

Some of the specified properties were farms in Badgall (235866) Treglasta (181863) Tregulland (195854) and Trenilk (226799) all these being listed on the current Ordnance Survey maps under the above grid references.

In this indenture George Sleeman is described as being "a yeoman of Egloskerry," and John Baron as "John Baron the younger of Treludick," and it would seem that they were all proposing to live together at Treludick. Perhaps George Sleeman was getting on in years and was approaching the age when he would need looking after, so what more natural that his daughter should live in the same house and be on hand when her father needed help. This would be a great relief to George for all old people dread the day when they can

Descent of Tregeare

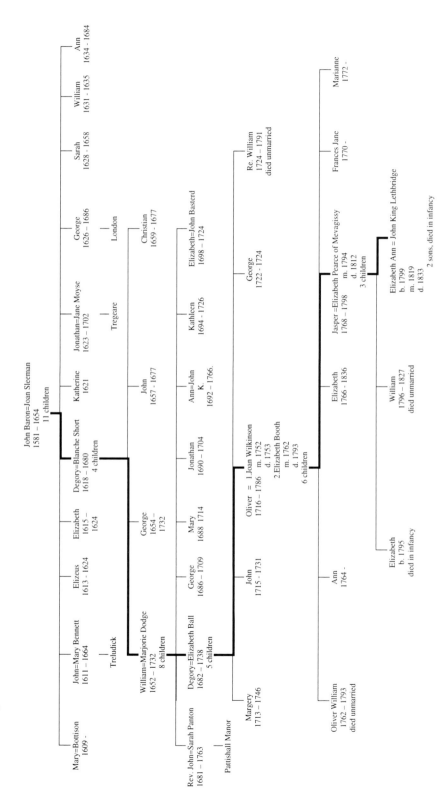

no more fend for themselves, when even the simple daily problems assume massive proportions, and the nights are full of terrors.

Four years after this settlement John Baron's Uncle John died and having no children of his own left his nephew further property, so that John and Joan Baron found themselves in increasingly affluent circumstances. After the birth of Katherine in 1621 came Jonathan in 1623 and George in 1626. A glance at the family tree will show that at this point John's eldest son John would be fifteen, his second son Degory eight and Jonathan three years old.

Custom and tradition indicated that in due course the eldest son would inherit the principal farm, the second son the next in importance, and so on, so that the chances of George the fourth son inheriting much wealth were not very great, hence it is not surprising to find that George, when he came of an age to leave school and start work, left home and was sent to London to make his fortune.

And make his fortune he did! He transformed the fortunes of the Baron family and lifted them from a family of well-to-do farmers into one with higher social and economic aspirations. The present Tregeare House and its many broad and pleasant acres are a testimonial to his affluence and care for his family, and a reminder of what became at its peak one of the largest estates in Cornwall.

George Baron was thirteen years old when his mother died, and it must have been about this time that he went to London, either as an apprentice or a trainee merchant, and embarked upon a career that in the next forty-five years brought him great wealth. When he was seventeen his father executed a deed granting him a share in the revenues of Treglista and Polmoutha and this no doubt was the foundation of his fortune for it was at this age that he would have been coming to the end of his apprenticeship.

His major trading appears to have been with Spain and particularly through the port of Bilbao, and it may be that he spent some time in that country as a young man, but further research might also uncover a connection with the East India Company which at this time was at the height of prosperity and was enabling many fortunes to be made by its traders.

In 1671 when George was forty-five he married an Elizabeth Howland aged thirty, of Streatham, who came of a family of wealthy merchants. In Queen Elizabeth's time Giles Howland had bought the manor of

Tooting Bec which included the village of Streatham. Giles' son John was Sheriff of Surrey and in 1681 his grandson, another John, married a daughter of Sir Josiah Child, Chairman of the East India Company, and their only daughter married a man whom later became the Duke of Bedford.

George acquired considerable property in the City and South London and as early as 1655 had bought the manor of Paris Gardens which extended from the river well into Southwark, the only trace of which left today is a Paris Gardens Road, and nearby a Cornwall Road and Duchy Road. His land also included Shakespeare's Globe Theatre and Bankside. On the north of the river he owned several properties in Great Wood Street including an inn, and also on Garlic Hill near the Mansion House. In 1666 he was inevitably involved in the Great Fire which started in Pudding Lane, only a few hundred yards from Garlic Hill. Many property owners suffered great losses in the fire, and how George Baron managed to avoid this is not known. An area of one hundred and thirty six acres stretching from the Tower to Temple Bar and containing an estimated thirteen thousand and two hundred houses and eighty nine churches was completely devastated.

The solution to this mystery must be that George Baron's property holdings in the City of London did not occur until after the Fire. A massive rebuilding programme took place in the devastated area and there were many opportunities for developers. Streets were widened and re-aligned and building was of brick rather than wood. Much that was old and out of date was eradicated, and as a result the growth of the City's business importance increased as never before. Merchants like George Baron who were there at this time and had an eye for the future took advantage of the situation and profited accordingly.

George Baron died in 1686 and his Will is a long and complicated document running to forty-eight pages. He had a lot of material possessions to leave and he went into great detail as to how his estates and the revenue for them should be distributed. He left his wife well provided for, leaving her his house, household furniture and effects, plate, jewels, coach, horses, and in cash £12,000, which in terms of todays debased currency would be equivalent to several million pounds. But above all George Baron was a family man. He left thirty legacies and annuities and did not appear to have forgotten anyone. Having no children of his own he remembered not only his brothers and sisters but also their children and their children's children.

He left money to several charities and to the poor, particularly of Egloskerry and of Bideford, the latter being a port in which he kept three ships involved in the trade with Spain. "£6 per annum to the poor seamen and their widows of Bideford, and £6 per annum to the bayzemakers of Barnstaple." The manufacture of baize cloth was a cottage industry in this part of Devon.

The three ships were probably Brigs, and were called "Bilbao Merchant", "Elizabeth" and "Bisra Merchant," and on their return voyages from Spain were used for importing wines. George Baron left a share in these ships to his "nephew" John Short who was his Agent in Bilbao. John was the son of Richard Short whose sister Blanche was married to Degory Baron, George's older brother. Another son of Richard Short, Jonathan, was also left a share in one of the ships, presumably because he too worked in Bilbao in the family business.

Yet another of George Baron's nephews was John Baron, son of his brother Jonathan, and this John figured importantly in George's Will, for after providing for all his kindred George turned his attention to the future and his Will contains the following clause.

> "I will and ordain and appoint that my executors therafter named shall within the term of eight years after my decease raise out of the rents and profits of my estate the sum of four thousand pounds of lawful money of England and the same so raised shall layout and bestow in the purchasing of lands of inheritance in such places as my said nephew John Baron shall counsel…"

The said nephew was in his middle twenties at the time and a student at Oxford University, and obviously George had a high regard for him. The Will is a complicated document as the following list of all the legacies and bequests will indicate. It was made in October 1685 and George Baron died in the following year.

List of Bequests etc. in George Baron's Will

1. £10 p.a. to the Rector of Egloskerry.

2. One shilling per week for bread to the poor of Egloskerry.

3. £10 p.a. to the master of the Free School at Launceston to teach ten poor children of the town and parish of Egloskerry.

4. £6 p.a. to the poor seamen and their widows of Bideford.

5. £6 p.a. to the poor bayzemakers and their widows of Barnstaple.

6. Two shillings per week to the poor widows and widowers of the parish of St. James Garlickhythe, London.

7. £12,000 to my wife Elizabeth.

8. All my plate, jewels, household goods, coach and coach horses (with some few exceptions) to my wife.

9. £20 p.a. to my sister Sarah Rowe.

10. £20 p.a. to William Rowe, husband of Sarah.

11. £200 to my niece Jessica Crodicott, daughter of William and Sarah Rowe, plus a further £100.

12. £100 each to Paul Rowe and William Rowe, sons of William and Sarah Rowe.

13. £300 each to Richard Bottison and Thomas Bottison, sons of my sister Mary Bottison.

14. £10 p.a. to the daughter of my sister Mary Bottison and now the wife of Thomas Goodman, and £300 to her child or children.

15. £300 to the maiden daughter of my sister Mary Bottison.

16. £10 p.a. to my niece, the sister of William Stanbury.

17. £300 to the children of my nephew William Stanbury, son of my late sister Ann Stanbury.

18. £300 to the children of my niece after her decease, with proviso.

19. £20 to my loving brother-in–law Richard Short.

20. £300 to William Short, eldest son of Richard Short.

21. To my nephew John Short, another son of Richard Short now at Bilbao one fourth part of the good ship BILBAO MERCHANT (Emmanuel Poke, Master), one half part of the good ship ELIZABETH (John Wild, Master) and one sixteenth part of the ship BISRA MERCHANT (Mr. Dover, Master), plus £400.

22. To my nephew Jonathan Short, another of the sons of Richard Short, three eighths part of the good ship ELIZABETH, plus £300.

23. £300 to the children of my niece Joan Chapman deceased.

24. £50 p.a. to my nephew John Baron, son of my brother Jonathan Baron and now a student at Oxford University, for eight years.

25. Within eight years of my decease my executors are to raise (out of the rents and profits of my estate) £4000 for the purchasing of lands of inheritance "in such places as my said nephew John Baron shall counsel," to be used by (a) the heirs of my body, and in default (b) my nephew John Baron, on trust of three persons during his life (c) first, second, third, fourth, fifth, sixth, seventh sons of John Baron, and in default of such issue (d) all and every daughter of John Baron and their heirs, and in default of such issue (e) any unborn child at the time of his death, and in default (f) William Baron my nephew, son of my brother Degory, then to William's son John, then to William's second son Degory, thence to Elizeus Baron.

26. £400 to my niece Sarah Baron.

27. £20 to my sister-in-law Blanche Baron. (Then he adds a proviso that if any of his properties in Shadwell are "impaired" all the above legatees, with the exception of his wife, shall proportionately share the loss.)

28. He appoints William Saltren of St. Ives and William Rowe (husband of his sister Sarah) as his Executors, and after all debts, expenses and legacies have been paid they shall then pay £100 per annum to Robert Baron (son of his eldest brother John) and £20 p.a. to his nephew Joseph Short.

29. The several charities mentioned above – i.e. Nos. 1, 2, 3, and 6 – shall be paid out of my property in Great Wood Street, London. Residue to (a) heirs of my body (b) my nephew Christopher Baron (c) first, second, third, fourth, fifth, sixth, seventh etc. sons of Christopher (d) any other unborn son (e) Robert Baron and his sons (f) John Baron and his sons (g) William Baron son of Degory Baron and his sons (h) my nephew Elizeus and his sons (i) the right heirs of George Baron.

Other heraditaments and promises (sic) of an estate of inheritance

(a) to my nephew William Baron, son of my brother Degory.

(b) then to William's first, second, third, fourth, fifth, sixth, seventh and all and everyson and sons...

(c) then to my nephew John Baron, son of Jonathan

(d) then to my nephew Christopher Baron, etc.

(e) then to my nephew Robert Baron, etc.

(f) then to Elizeus Baron

(g) then to the right heirs of George Baron forever.

He then lays down guide lines to the trustees for the purchase of "freehold lands and tenements of inheritance in fee simple in the realm of England" to be approved by Christopher and William Baron, sons of his brother Degory, or the survivor of them. Then follows detail on granting of leases, and other matters, and reiteration of the necessary approval of Christopher and William Baron.

30.   Finally, £10 to William Saltern to buy him a ring.

Signed and sealed by George Baron
On 9th October 1685.
(On forty-eight sheets of paper)

It can readily be seen from the above list of bequests that George Baron had amassed a considerable fortune, and that he was desperately anxious that his branch of the Baron family should benefit thereby. It must have been a great sadness to him that he had no children of his own, and his surviving nephews and nieces had much to be thankful for. His beneficence altered many people's lives and led directly to the founding of the Tregeare estate.

A fine portrait of George Baron hangs in the dining room at Treludick, his birthplace. In his hand is a sealed envelope; does this perhaps contain his plans for the future?

IN SUNDRY PLACES

Chapter 7 - The Family Divides

At the time when George Baron was sent to London to seek his fortune other changes were taking place at Treludick. John Baron was fifty six years old and Joan was possibly not yet fifty but was already suffering from the effects of having so many children and was struggling to manage a busy household that contained at least nine people.

Her first child Mary, born in 1609, was already married to a man called Botteson, and was presumably no longer living at home, but most of her other children would still be under her care. In 1637 her eldest son John was twenty six and was on the point of getting married, her next boy Elizeus would have been twenty four had he lived but he had died at the age of eleven. A daughter Elizabeth, two years younger, had also died in 1624 in the same year as her brother, and one wonders about the circumstances of this little family tragedy. To the mother the loss of two of her children at the same time can be a devastating blow.

The working farmyard

Her next boy Degory was nineteen, and had no doubt been working on the farm with his father for several years. The next child Katherine was sixteen and already of an age to take a full share in the running of the household along with her mother. Then came Jonathan at thirteen, George at eleven, Sarah nine, and Ann three. Another boy William had died the year before at the age of four. No wonder poor Joan was worn out, her life was hard and unrelenting, and yet it was typical of hundreds of farmer's wives who were forced to bear many children and consequently had the responsibility of feeding many mouths.

The family were also about to be enlarged by young John's marriage to Mary Bennett of Hexworthy, who would be an addition to the number of people already living in the house. But other, and equally fundamental changes were in the air. In 1639 Joan Baron died, George had left home, and the responsibility of management of the household devolved on young John and Mary, and with new young people in charge new ideas began to emerge.

One of the first things they decided was that the Treludick house was too old and too decrepit, and possibly not large enough to house a big family, and that the only thing to do was to rebuild it in a more modern manner and make it something they could be proud of, something that would last for a hundred years or more. And this they certainly achieved for the house they built is still with us today and is rightly regarded as a thing of beauty, well worth preserving.

The house is of modified Elizabethan design, and that is to say it consists of a long central section with wings at each end, but in this instance the wing at the southerly end is a long one. The front faces east with a central front door, and there are two stories only. Immediately to the north of the house is a large barn, and the lintel over the door of this building is carved with the initials "J. B." and "M. B", and the date 1641.

The house is now three hundred and fifty years old, which is in itself a tribute to its rugged construction and though obviously it has been modernised and brought up to date, it is basically the same building it was in 1641. There is another date carved on the barn door, 1862, which implies a major restoration, and one wonders if it was at this comparatively recent date that modern sanitation was introduced. It is difficult for us to believe now that when the house was built, and for its first 250 years there would have been no indoor supply of running water, and no sanitation whatsoever. The only loo would have been an earth closet outside at the back of the house, and possibly some way away from it, the only water for washing or drinking would come from the well. No wonder that hygiene was so lacking, and infant mortality was so great. In our centrally heated houses today where we can flood a room with light at the touch of a switch, and where we have a piped supply of drinking water, we tend to forget that these modern luxuries did not become possible until the beginning of the twentieth century.

You enter the house through its stone porch which was designed to keep out the weather when it was easterly, and the outer stone archway has a moulding round the top with hollow chamfers, a feature that suggests the archway is older than the 1640's, and one wonders whether it may have come from the earlier house. The flight of stairs is broken by a mezzanine landing lit by a small window facing west, and this window is glazed by a chequered design of coloured glass which in the evening when the sun is low fills the hall with coloured light.

The massive front door

Front of Treludick

View to east from the house

The front porch.
Note Insurance Company badge

As in many buildings of this period the principal rooms lead off the hall and are inter-connected with other rooms. All these ground floor rooms are of good size and have low ceilings and exposed oak beams. The dining room on the right, and in which the portrait of George Baron hangs, is panelled from floor to ceiling and has very satisfying proportions. Another feature which is frequently found in seventeenth century farmhouses is an additional staircase at each end of the building, and it has been suggested that these end staircases, and the fact that all rooms were provided with two doors, is an indication that farmhouses were invariably used as centres for dealing in contraband.

Treludick is surrounded by typical undulating Cornish farmland, and its nearest neighbours are Trebeath nearly half a mile away to the south-east, and Treburtle the same distance in the opposite direction. The ground slopes away from the front of the house down to a little stream which is a tributary of the River Ottery only half a mile away to the north. This stream contains a small lake which the present owners, Percy and Marion Uglow, remember in their earlier years was annually increased in size by damming the stream. The resulting head of water was then allowed to power a water wheel which with suitable shafting operated the farm machinery. The name Treludick has indeed been interpreted as meaning 'the town of the lake' or of 'the bosom of the waters'.

In 1647 Degory Baron, the second son of John and Joan was twenty nine years old and he too got married. His bride was Blanche Short who is believed to have come from North Petherwin, a charming village about a couple of miles north of Egloskerry and at one time just inside the borders of Devonshire. Living at Treludick at this time would be John and Mary Baron and three of their children, plus John's father who was now sixty six, and probably Sarah aged nineteen and Ann aged thirteen. John's two other brothers Degory (twenty nine) and Jonathan (twenty four) could possibly still have been living at home, but there is little doubt that Degory at any rate would be moving to set up his own household now he was getting married, and the records show that he moved to Tregeare. Which farm he moved to is not clear, but there were two possibilities, Home Farm and Tregeare Farm, the little hamlet itself being called South Tregeare to distinguish it from North Tregeare (map reference 228884).

The records show that John and Mary Baron ultimately had eight children, and it is interesting to note that in the south wing at Treludick is a very large bedroom which could well have been a dormitory for several children, and when they built the house in 1641 this was obviously a consideration that had to be borne in mind. At the present time this room is used for storing apples and is full of their distinctive fragrance.

John Baron died in 1664 and an Inventory of his goods and chattels was made by those close relations of his, Richard Short the brother of Blanche who had married John's brother Degory, William Rowe the husband of his sister Sarah, and his brother Degory himself. It is an interesting document, (see page 69) not only in the variety of the household effects that he owned and their rather basic nature, but also many missing items which today we consider essential and take for granted but which he obviously did not have.

A pre-1915 picture, before the shrubs had grown

For instance there is no mention of curtains, and all his carpets and cushions were together valued at only £1-10-0d. There was no crockery or cutlery listed, and no such things as easy chairs. Indeed, there are only six timber chairs listed and ten joint stools, valued at

Portrait of George Baron
1626 – 1686

Left:
Over the Barn door
the initials JB and
MB

Right:
Multi coloured
stair window

Left:
Splendid dining
room door

Right:
Panelling upstairs.
The blank panel
was once a
window to let light
in from the
bedroom

£2, but on the other hand eight feather mattresses which were obviously regarded as a luxury at £22-6-8, or £2.78 each. The total inventory of £722-16-4 indicates that he was a very successful man, the majority of this sum coming from his farm stock and crops and from two leases that he owned. In this Inventory John Baron is, for the first time, described as 'a gentleman'.

At John's death his eldest son Christopher aged twenty five inherited, though it is possible he had been living there all his life. Christopher married in 1673 but had no son to succeed him, and in 1684 his daughter Joane married a John Saltern who was her cousin and she was the last Baron to live at Treludick. A family tree showing the descent of Teludick down to the present day is shown on page 70.

Moulded plaster ceiling
in dining room

John Baron's Inventory 1664

An Inventory indented of the goods and chattells of JOHN BARON, late of Treludick in the County of Cornwall, gentleman deceased made and priced by William Rowe, Richard Short and Degory Baron the nine and twentieth day of December in the Sixteenth year of the reign of our Sovereign Lord Charles by the grace of God and England. Anno domini 1664.

Imprimis in ready money		£30
ITEM due to him upon specialtion		£20
ITEM his plate		£12
ITEM his apparell		£10
ITEM his books		£1
ITEM two chattell leases		£111
ITEM eight featherbeds performed		£22-6-8
ITEM four duft beds performed		£3
ITEM three bedsteads with their furniture		£4
ITEM two other bedsteads with testers		£1-6-8
ITEM bedsteads and six tressell bedsteads		£3
ITEM fifteen brass pans great and small		£14
ITEM five brass pots, two brass culdrons one brass skillett, two chaisin dishes		£4
ITEM six brass candlesticks		£1
ITEM four dozen of pewter dishes and three flagons		£4-10-0
ITEM Six pewter saucers, one pewter basin and ewer and four pewter chamber pots		£13-0-4
ITEM six table boards and four livery tables		£4
ITEM six timber chairs and ten joint stools		£2
ITEM two press cupboards and three forms		£1-0-2
ITEM one spruce chest three other timber chests and one trunk		£4
ITEM five table cloths, two dozen of table napkins and other linen		£2-0-10
ITEM eleven oxen		£64

ITEM two bulls and sixteen kine		£50
ITEM thirty–nine heifers and steeres of two and three years old		£70
ITEM twenty–five yearlings and calves		£19
ITEM Seventeen horses, mares, and colts		£34
ITEM two hundred and ninety eight sheep		£55
ITEM twenty-three swine hogs		£10
ITEM his poultry		20/-
ITEM four hogsheads, nine barrells, six keiver and other timber vessels		£3
ITEM a pair of brass handirons		20/-
ITEM four spits and dripping pans and other household stuff of iron		13/4
ITEM his corn in the mowhay		£50
ITEM fourteen acres of wheat in the ground		£21
ITEM two wagons and three butts		27/-
ITEM three pair of wheels with four axalls and two pair of old broken wheels		£12
ITEM his plough stuff and other 'implements of husbandry'		60/-
ITEM his hay		60/-
ITEM his timber and timber stuff		£3
ITEM his saddles, bridles and other furniture for horses		£1-6-8
ITEM his carpets and cushions		£1-10-0
ITEM five stone troughs with the provisions for the house		£5-6-8
ITEM all other things of small value not particularly mentioned or priced		50/-
TOTAL		£722-16-4

Richard Short
William Rowe
Degory Baron

Descent of Treludick

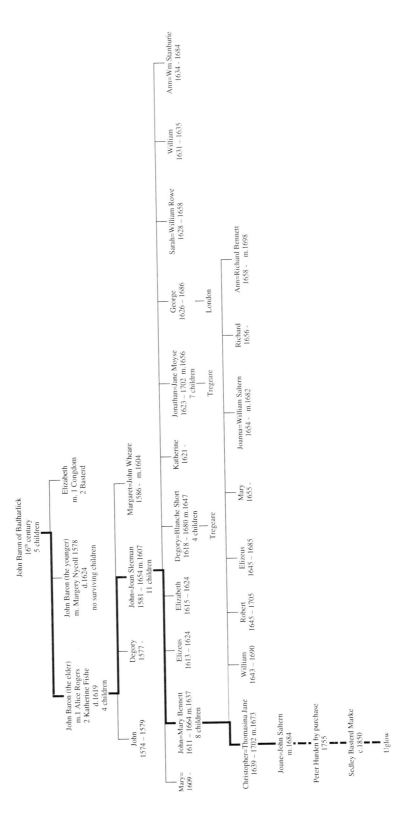

John Baron of Badharlick
16th century
5 children

John Baron (the elder)
m. 1 Alice Rogers
2 Katherine Fishe
d.1619
4 children

John Baron (the younger)
m. Margery Nycoll 1578
d.1624
no surviving children

Elizabeth
m. 1 Congdom
2 Basterd

John
1574 – 1579

Degory
1577 -

John=Joan Sleeman
1581 – 1654 m.1607
11 children

Margaret=John Wheare
1586 - m.1604

Mary=
1609 -

Elizeus
1613 – 1624

Elizabeth
1615 – 1624

Degory=Blanche Short
1618 – 1680 m.1647
4 children
Tregeare

Katherine
1621 -

Jonathan=Jane Moyse
1623 – 1702 m.1656
7 children
Tregeare

George
1626 – 1686
London

Sarah=William Rowe
1628 – 1658

William
1631 – 1635

Ann=Wm Stanburie
1634 - 1684

John=Mary Bennett
1611 – 1664 m.1637
8 children

William
1643 – 1690

Robert
1645 – 1705

Elizeus
1645 – 1685

Mary
1655 -

Joanna=William Saltern
1654 - m.1682

Richard
1656 -

Ann=Richard Bennett
1658 - m.1698

Christopher=Thomasina Jane
1639 – 1702 m.1673

Joane=John Saltern
m.1684

Peter Hurden by purchase
1755

Sedley Basterd Marke
c.1850

Uglow

IN SUNDRY PLACES

Chapter 8 - Old Tregeare

The last chapter showed how the large family of John Baron and his wife Joan Sleeman developed, and how his four surviving sons ultimately went their own ways in search of fame and fortune. Only one of them, George, failed to become a farmer, but indeed he was the only one to acquire great wealth. However, the family were also on their way climbing the ladder of social success, and when their eldest son John, who married Mary Bennett, died in 1664 he was described on the Inventory of his goods as a gentleman.

The other two boys, Degory and Jonathan, both appear to have moved to farms in neighbouring Tregeare and we must follow them there. It is difficult to say for certain which farms they went to, though probably Degory, as the elder, would go to Tregeare Farm, and Jonathan would take Home Farm. But there are other farms in the district that are possibilities, notably Lidcot and High Hall, both of which at some time came into the possession of the Baron family.

And while the inevitable changes were taking place another building and another family were making their mark on Tregeare. The building has now long since disappeared but its site is known and it is still remembered and talked about, for it was a gentleman's residence and a cut above the usual farmhouse in the area. Records refer to it as the Old Tregeare Mansion House, and its position was overlooking the little village green, at map reference 243867. The site is no longer marked on Ordnance Survey maps.

Old Tregeare Mansion House is believed to have been built in 1582, and though there is no sign of it today, the evidence of its existence is contained in an impressive stone archway or doorway that has survived. This is reputed to have been the original front door of the old mansion, and the triangular spandrels on either side of the arch contain the initials L. B. and the date 1582. Architecturally this is logical and in keeping with the doorway of a prestigious small country house of the late 16th century.

The initials L. B. at first quite naturally suggest that the house was built by a Baron, but research into the church baptismal registers has failed to produce any member of the family who was given a Christian name beginning with 'L'. But there is another family, prominent in the neighbourhood at this time, whose name also began with 'B', this being the Bligh family.

Bligh is a well known name in North Cornwall and there are records spelling it in various ways – Blighe, Blight, and even Bleyeh and Bllight – the most prevalent versions today being Blight, Blythe and Bligh. There are records of Blighs living at Bodwin, Botathan, St. Tudy, Egloskerry and Tregeare, and the Blighs of Egloskerry were for many years Stewards of Penheale Manor. Lake's History says their 'seat' was at little Penheale, which was not far from Tregeare,

at West Downend. Perhaps their most famous son was Captain William Bligh, born in St. Tudy in 1754, who in his naval career suffered mutiny in his ship the Bounty and was cast adrift in an open boat. He survived this ignominy and later became Governor of New South Wales, though three years later in 1808 he was forcibly deposed, which suggests that it was not only Fletcher Christian and his seven mutineers who could not stand the sight of him.

The first two Ordnance Survey Maps demonstrate the disappearance of the Old Tregeare Mansion House

In Tregeare there is a record of a Leonard Bligh who died in 1583, and he is the most likely man to have built the Old Tregeare Mansion House and left his initials on the doorway. Unfortunately his Will has disappeared, for this might have told us something about the house but there is a record of George the son of John Bligh of Tregeare who died in 1586, and of John Bligh himself who died in 1608 and is described as a gentleman. There is also a Will and Inventory of an Anthony Bligh of Tregeare, gentleman, who died early in 1635, which date clashes with the information that three generations of the Edgcombe family were living at Tregeare from around 1630 to 1740.

25" 0.S 2nd Edition
1906

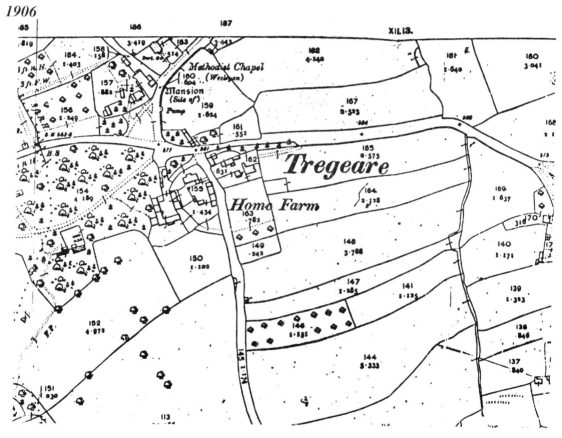

There is a slight discrepancy in the dates here for both families could not have been living at Old Tregeare between 1630 and 1635, but it would seem definite that Anthony Bligh was in residence until he died on 1 April 1635. His Will describes him as a gentleman and it is unlikely that there would have been another gentleman's house in Tregeare of a sufficient quality to attract a member of the Edgcombe family.

The Edgcombes were already established in Laneast having acquired the manor from the Arundells whom at one time were the wealthiest and most powerful family in Cornwall. There is a record of a Roger Edgcombe marrying a Katherine Lay, a widow, in 1624, and another marriage between Roger Edgcombe and Julian Rubbie in 1637, followed by a third marriage when Roger Edgcombe married Jane Stroute of Egloskerry on 22 April 1639. If this is the same Roger Edgcombe he was obviously not having much luck with his wives, though in fact Roger and Jane did father a son, another Roger, and this son lived at Old Tregeare, dying in 1677. The Will and Inventory of this latter Roger are available, and extracts from these documents are included at the end of this Chapter. The size of Old Tregeare may be estimated by the fact that in 1662 Roger Edgcombe was paying tax on sixteen hearths.

The Hearth Tax Records certainly suggest that Roger Edgcombe was in possession of Old Tregeare in 1662 since there does not appear to have been any other home in the neighbourhood that could claim as many as sixteen working hearths. Perhaps the Edgcombes bought Old Tregeare from the Blighs, possibly on the demise of Anthony Bligh in 1635.

In his Will Anthony Bligh appoints his brother John of Bratton Clovelly in Devon as his executor, and mentions two sisters Elizabeth and Ann, and another brother Nevill, but no mention of a wife. Nor is there any mention of Old Tregeare, in fact the only property listed is "all those messuage, lande and tenemente situate and being in Polsue.....within the parishe of Jacobstow." And this is only mentioned as security for a legacy of one hundred pounds to his sister Elizabeth. The rest of the Will merely covers two further bequests of twenty pounds each, forty shillings to the poor of Egloskerry, and ten shillings to the preacher of his funeral sermon.

The Will of Roger Edgcombe in 1677 is also a curious document and similarly uncommunicative in that it makes no mention of any property. It also poses another problem – it describes Roger Edgcombe as being of Landeast in the County of Cornwall. One can forgive the scribe for the odd 'd' that has crept into Laneast, but Old Tregeare is actually in the parish of Egloskerry and in a legal document Roger should have been described as of this latter parish.

The Edgcombes of course achieved considerable national prominence, their seat in the south east extremity of Cornwall being originally Cotehele, from whence they built and moved into Mount Edgcombe.

The latter has been described as one of the finest parks in the country and in the 19th century became famous for its house parties which were attended by many visiting members of the aristocracy and the Royal Family. Celebrated visitors included the Prince and Princess of Wales, later King Edward VII and Queen Alexandra, and it was rumoured that the expense of this style of entertaining ultimately caught up with the Edgcombes who were constrained to close Mount Edgcombe in the winter months and move across the River Tamar into their Winter Villa in Stonehouse. Mount Edgcombe was very seriously damaged by an incendiary bomb on 22 April 1941, and Stonehouse, which is part of Devonport, was demolished in 1955. Many photographs of Mount Edgcombe House and its grounds survive, one of the features of the latter being a forty-foot high Ilex hedge which in the 19th century took two men a month to clip.

Old Tregeare has left one or two other tangible reminders of its existence besides the stone doorway mentioned above, which since 1900 has been situated in the kitchen garden of the present house, between the two greenhouses. There are two stone mullioned windows flanked by large gateposts immediately behind the house, also erected in 1900, as were one or two items set up in the grounds near the Pond. These included another granite doorway, a window, and remnants of a granite chimney, the latter having been used as the steps into the pond.

The fine Settle built from oak from Old Tregeare

Another relic of Old Tregeare is at present at Treludick, this being a rather splendid three piece suite carved in oak and comprising a settle

75

and two matching armchairs. The back of the settle bears the initials W. B. and the date 1750. Mr. Percy Uglow, the owner, claims that some time in the first half of the 18th century Old Tregeare suffered a disastrous fire, the only part of the building to survive being the oak doors from which this furniture was subsequently made.

There is little doubt that this settle and armchairs did once belong to the Baron family for there is in existence an old photograph showing them installed in the hall of the present Tregeare House, from whence they were purchased by Mr. Uglow at an auction sale in 1981. But the Old Tregeare Mansion House was still habitable in 1801 for the estate accounts for that year list Miss Ann Baron as living there at a rent of ten pounds per annum, and it is not until September 1900 that it was finally demolished.

Corroborative evidence comes in the shape of the first two editions of the 25 inch to the mile Ordnance Survey Maps. In the first issue dated 1884 is the outline of a building on this particular spot, bearing the legend "Mansion: (Remains of)" and in the second edition of 1906 this outline has been replaced by a simple cross and the notice "Mansion: (Site of)."

Remains of Old Tregeare converted into cottages

As in the case of many old buildings the last few years of Old Tregeare tell a sad story. A further old photograph which can be dated between 1870 and 1875 shows a building on the site, and though by no stretch of the imagination can this be described as an Elizabethan Mansion House it must indeed be all that was left of the old building at that time. A family record says that as soon as the new Tregeare House was completed (c. 1820 – 1830) the old one, or what was left of it, was converted into farm cottages, and for the rest of its life it did at least fulfil a useful purpose.

Roger Edgcombe's Will and Inventory 1677

His Will contained eight items only, the first committing his soul to God Almighty and his body to Christian burial. The next six were bequests of two hundred pounds to each of six of his children Jane, Joane, John, Grace, Richard, and William, these legacies to be paid to each of them on attaining the age of eighteen.

In the final item he left the rest of his goods and chattels to his wife Grace and his son Roger, appointed them joint executors, and charged them with the maintenance of the above children until they reached the age of eighteen.

His Will was made on Friday 18th May 1677 and proved on 2nd July the same year.

The Inventory of his goods, chattels and credits was taken on 13th June 1677 and included forty-seven items ranging in value from twelve shillings to five hundred and eighty pounds. Items of ten pounds and over are listed below and give an indication of relative values in the middle of the 17th century. The total value of his Inventory amounted to £1212-10-1d.

His purse, girdle and wearing apparrill	40-10-00	corn in the Mowhay	10-00-00
5 – 3 year old steers	14-00-00	8 acres of wheat and rye	16-00-00
10 oxen	40-00-00	15 acres of oats and barley	22-10-00
7 steers of 2 year old	14-00-00	3 pairs of wheels a Butt and wain with iron axles	10-00-00
9 cows and 1 bull	30-00-00	8 beds performed with bolsters blankets	30-00-00
9 cows on the lease (?)	29-00-05		
4 cows 2 steers and 1 Gote (?)	22-00-00	10 brass pans	12-10-06
12 yearlings	15-00-00	debts owing upon spicialby (?)	160-00-00
10 calfes	10-00-00	in despirate debts	10-00-00
191 wethers and ewes	36-00-00	All his chattle estates	580-00-00
12 horses and colts	30-00-00	**Total**	**£1212-10-01**

IN SUNDRY PLACES

Chapter 9 - The Tregeare Farms

At the age of twenty nine Degory Baron had married Blanche Short of North Petherwin, and it was then that they probably moved to Tregeare. The date was February 1647, but the Baron ownership of a "messuage" in South Tregeare had occurred nineteen years previously in 1628 when his grandfather John had acquired it in 1576 from the Lord of the Manor of Penheale, George Grenville. It is pure supposition that it was in 1647 that Degory and Blanche moved to Tregeare, but what a magnificent wedding present this would have been.

His father was well able to start the young couple off in this way for his own fortunes were flourishing. His farm at Treludick was prospering, and his eldest son John who would succeed him at Treludick was already well in the saddle and in control. In fact, at sixty six years of age John Baron was probably already finding it possible to take things a little easier and enjoy the fruits of his many years of hard work.

On the national stage at this time a fundamental drama was reaching its climax and disruptive changes were on the way. Charles 1 was still on the throne but his position was becoming increasingly unstable and within the next two years he would have to cope with treatment by his Parliament that was without precedent. This confrontation had divided the country into two distinct parties, on one hand those who were appalled at the thought of challenging the right of the King to rule, and on the other those who saw the opportunity for long needed changes and the possibility of power devolving on the people.

In country districts the effects of this quarrel were not as violent as in the towns, and this was particularly true of Cornwall which was a long way from the centre of the trouble in Westminster. But there were local problems. The gentry in general, and this included Paul Speccott, Lord of the Manor of Penheale, as well as some of the biggest families in the South West, were Royalist and loyal to the Crown, but at Treludick for example Mary Bennett, John Baron's wife, came of a family that was fiercely in favour of the Parliament's cause, her brother being Colonel Robert Bennett, a leading Parliamentary figure and administrator, based in Launceston.

In the name of God Amen the fifteenth day of November
in the yeare of our Lord One Thousand Six hundred and Eightie
I Degory Baron of Egloskerry in the County of Cornwall gent
being of sound and perfect memory (praised be god for the same) I
doe make and ordaine this my last will and Testament. I command
my soule into the hands of god who gave it mee, and my body unto
Christian buriall, Touching my goods and chattells I give and
dispose as followeth: Imprimis I give and bequeath unto Blanch
my wife the Moytie or halfendeale of all my stock and goods
Quick and dead within doores and without of what nature & quality
soever the same be, To have and to hold the same my said wife for and
during the tearme of her Naturall life, And my will and meaning
is that att her decease shee shall leave the same to my Executour
hereafter named in the same or as good a condition as shee shall
find them att the tyme of my decease. Item I give unto the said Blanch
my wife the Summe of fiftie pounds to be paid her by my Executour
att the end of halfe a yeare next after my decease And if my said wife
happen to dye before the said fiftie pounds become due to be paid, then
my Executor shall pay the same to such one or ones as my said
wife shall appoint by her last will. Item I give and bequeath
unto Margery Launder of the parish of Tresmeere in the County
aforesaid twentie shillings, and to her brother Jeremiah
Launder five shillings, Item I give unto Sibilla Hodge which is
now a servant to mee Ten shillings, these three last Legacies to be
paid within one monthe after my death, Item I give unto Peter
Colmer who is now an apprentice to mee Twentie shillings to be paid
him when he shall accomplish the age of One and Twentie yeares.
Item I give unto the poor of the parish of Egloskerry fortie shillings:
And I doe hereby make and ordaine William Baron my sonne sole
Executor of this my last will and Testament, And I doe hereby revoke
and annull all former wills: In witness whereof I have subscribed
my name and sett my Seale unto this my present last will & Testament
the daie and yeare first above written.

Signed sealed published and declared
by the said Degory Baron to be his last
will and Testament in presence of

Chris Baron
Johan Baron

Gregory Baron

The marke of Andrew Rogers

Degory Baron's Will 1680. *Courtesy of Cornish Record Office.*

The fighting in Cornwall virtually came to an end in 1645 as the Parliamentarians gradually came out on top, and no one could have been more grateful than the farmers of the Baron family, for they were busy building up their little agricultural empire, and fighting and farming do not mix. If the truth were to be known it is possible that the overwhelming wish amongst all the ordinary country folk was that both sides would go away so that everyone could get on with their life again in peace.

Degory and Blanche had four children in all, but their first born William did not arrive until 1652, five years after their marriage. It is tempting to suggest they were waiting to begin their family until the war was over and a more stable regime had been established, but five years is a long time and even at the time of the wedding it was apparent that Parliament was going to win. Perhaps it was that they wanted to spend a few years building up the farm without the added responsibility of children.

But there is of course another possible cause, namely the natural one that they were unable for a time to have the children they desired. If this was indeed the case then Degory was probably justifiably worried since he had come of a large family of eleven, though at least three of this family had died in childhood. And this inevitably raises another worry. Child mortality was high in the 17th century, and was expected, but subsequent events seemed to suggest the possibility of their being some sort of genetic weakness creeping into the Baron family.

Their remaining three children arrived regularly at two to three year intervals, but none of them lived to adulthood. George was born in 1654 and died in 1655, John was born in 1657 and died in 1662. Christian the fourth child (and a daughter) certainly lived a little longer, but died in 1677 at the age of eighteen. Losing three children out of four must have been a very heavy blow to Degory, and particularly to Blanche, their mother, and the loss of her only daughter in the full flush of womanhood no doubt struck Blanche as an especially savage blow. Her life during the remaining twenty two years must have seemed strangely empty.

Degory's Will and his Inventory have survived and it is interesting to compare them with those of his elder brother John who died sixteen years earlier in 1664. Perhaps it is unfair to compare Tregeare too closely with Treludick, for after all the latter was an established estate that had been growing in importance for years, whereas the farm at Tregeare was a relatively recent acquisition and at this time its future could only be conjectured.

An Inventory indented of the goods chattells and
Debts of [...] Baron late of [...] in the
countie off Cornwall [...] deceased made and prised
the [...] day off December in the yeare of our Lord
One Thousand Six hundred and eighty [...] by Christopher
Baron, William Rowe, & Richard [...], as followeth.

Imprimis his purse and girdle & wearing apparell —

Item in ready mony.
Item due to him upon Specialties
Item Desperate Debts
Item Two featherbeds —
Item Two featherbolster —
Item four paire of Blanckets —
Item five paire of Sheetes —
Item his Table linnin
Item five Coverletts
Item Three bedsteads with Testers —
Item one Trundell bedstead —
Item one dozen off pewter dishes
   and six pewter plates
Item one pewter flagon and other small pewter —
Item five brass pannes great and small —
Item Two brass potts —
Item one brass skillet two brass
   candlesticks, and other brass
Item a Spitt a dripping pann and other
   household stuff of Iron
Item Three Tableboards, three formes
   chaires, five joynd stooles and one fforme
Item one Timber Presse, one Twanell
   and two cofferes. —
Item his corne in his Mowhay —
Item Three Loads off Wheat —
Item six paire off wheeles and one waine —
Item his plough stuff, & other implem[en]ts off husbandry
Item Dayrie Lidies, & other Timber vessells —
Item his Timber unwrought —
Item one Musket and one Sword —
Item his oxen, cowes, and other young
   cattle being in all Twenty —
Item Three swine
Item Seaventy five sheepe —
Item five horses —

The Inventory of his goods.
Note 'one musket and one
sword'.
Courtesy of Cornish Record Office.

81

Obviously Treludick was very much the bigger and in stock alone it dwarfed its newer neighbour. In John Baron's inventory are listed eleven oxen, two bulls and sixteen kine, thirty nine heifers and steers, twenty five yearlings and calves, two hundred and ninety eight sheep, and a rather surprising figure of seventeen horses mares and colts, the total value of this collection being put at £292. In the Tregeare Inventory a few years later the similar items included "his oxen, cowes and other young cattle being in all twenty" plus three horses and seventy five sheep at a total value of under £60.

In household goods and domestic chattels the difference was equally great, as for example at Treludick the inventory included fifteen brass pans great and small, as compared with five at Tregeare. One item that was obviously greatly prized was the featherbed, there being eight at Treludick, valued at £22-6-8 and two at Tregeare at £5-0-0.

One other item, of passing interest, which appears only on the Tregeare inventory is "one musket and one sword – 12 shillings," the strange thing about this entry being that it was John's wife Mary Bennett at Treludick who was related to Robert Bennett a leading local Parliamentarian. But perhaps these items were purely souvenirs of the Civil War that had been over for many many years.

William and Marjorie had eight children in all and there was no infant mortality, though four of them died at a comparatively early age. But their first child, John, lived to be eighty two, and under him an entirely new branch of the Baron family was founded. The normal procedure was for the eldest son to inherit the property owned by his father but in this instance John did not become a farmer but entered the Church. Obviously this sets him slightly apart from the rest of the Barons, and gives him an added interest, and it is with him that a major change in the history of the Barons of Tregeare takes place.

Indeed it takes a little time to appreciate the full significance of what is happening at this point. John Baron is making a complete break with tradition and the pattern of centuries, and aided and abetted by his younger brother Degory he is paving the way for the establishment of present – day South Tregeare. Within the next hundred years the Tregeare Estate is destined to become one of the largest and finest in Cornwall, and its house and surroundings a shining example of small country house architecture at its best.

It has been suggested that the change began with William Baron, the Rev. John Baron's father, and this may well be so. Certainly the details have been somewhat smudged by time but these are relatively unimportant, and in looking for the 'fons et origo' of such a fundamental change of direction we have of course to go back to the Will of William Baron's wealthy Uncle George.

It will be remembered (see page 55) that in his Will George Baron left instructions that within eight years of his death a large sum of money was to be raised with the object of purchasing "estates of inheritance" which would ensure the establishment and continuation of the Baron family fortunes. George died in 1686 so that in theory this fund would have been available as from 1692.

Further research will be necessary to determine when and if William Baron made use of this money, and also to establish just how involved William was in his Uncle's business, for it must not be assumed that as soon as George died his entreprenurial activities in the City and South London would come to an end. One does not abandon a gold mine when the proprietor dies. But as far as we are concerned the money certainly became available and subsequent thinking and planning was affected thereby.

William gave his eldest son a good education and sent him to Exeter College, Oxford, where he matriculated in 1697 at the age of seventeen. Later, in 1703, he became Chaplain Fellow of Exeter College, a position he held for ten years, and he also acquired a vicarage in Cornwall which he held from 1705 to 1722 though it would not seem that he ever became resident. In 1720 John married Sarah Panton at St. James' church, Aldgate, being described in the church register as "of Wanstead" and he certainly maintained very close links with London for the rest of his life.

In 1730 the Rev. John's mother Marjorie died and in the same year he purchased, for £6000, two manors at Pattishall in Northamptonshire. Where the money came from is not specified, but no doubt the main source was George Baron's Estates of Inheritance Fund.

Two years later in 1732 William Baron died and Rev. John inherited more property which had originated in his Uncle George's Paris Gardens Estate in London. At this point it is interesting to take a backward glance at the Will of Elizabeth Baron, Uncle George's widow, who died in 1712, as one or two extracts from her Will give an indication of the extraordinary amount of wealth that was being distributed at this time.

Her largest legacy was one of £3000 to Her Grace Elizabeth, the Duchess of Bedford, to whom she was related, and to the Duchess's daughters Lady Rachel Russell and Lady Elizabeth Russell, "to each one a row of my pearls." Among numerous smaller legacies was one–

> "To my cousin William Baron of Tregeare in Cornwall £100 and to Marjery his wife and his two sons and four daughters each £10 and to each of the latter one row of my gold chain."

Another legacy was –

> "To my cousin Anne Bennett £50 and her Uncle George Baron's little picture set in gold and to her son ten guineas and to her daughters Ann and Thomasin each one row of my gold chain."

To three other girls, daughter of her cousin Joanna Saltern, she also left to each one row of her gold chain, an indication that it must have been quite a considerable chain.

Another bequest concerned property and read as follows –

> "To my sister Suzanna Lettern for 12 years my remainder of the lease of the house in which I dwell also other houses on Garlicke Hill and a house in Bread Street and after 12 years I give said house in which I dwell to my cousin John Baron, Fellow of Exeter College and the issue of his body, remainder to his brother Degory Baron and his heirs."

The Rev. John Baron continued to live in London, some at least of his children were born there, and his links with Cornwall became more and more tenuous. One friendship he maintained was with Arthur Squire of High Hall near Tregeare who died in 1733. The Squires had owned High Hall for over a hundred years and was an important family in Laneast parish, an indication of this being that in the Hearth Tax records of 1662 John Squire was paying on seven hearths, the largest number in the parish.

But Arthur Squire died in the parish of Westminster and it is interesting that he left all his property to Rev. John Baron of Wanstead, Essex to sell at the best rate and honour a number of legacies, two of which incidentally were to other reverend gentlemen, and one to a John

Adams who was left £50 on condition that he repaid an outstanding debt of £100. One wonders if John Adams lived at the neighbouring farm of Lidcott, in which case he would have been an ancestor of Laneast's most famous son the eminent astronomer and mathematician John Couch Adams who was born at Lidcott in 1819.

The big change in direction of the Baron history took place in 1732 when William Baron died and his Cornish properties were taken over, not by his traditional son and heir but by his second son, Degory. It is clear that this was an amicable and business like arrangement for before he died William executed a long and rather complicated deed designed to ensure that Degory would in fact inherit the intended property, and that Rev. John would pay to his brother the sum or sums of money due to him from the estate of his Uncle George. In this deed William refers to his own last Will and testament that was dated 20 September 1714, a date that in view of the demise of George Baron's widow in 1712 may have some significance. As from this time the future development and possible rebuilding of the South Tregeare property was assured.

IN SUNDRY PLACES

Chapter 10 - Problems

When William Baron died in 1732 the inheritance situation at first sight seems perfectly clear. His eldest son the Rev. John had struck out in a new direction and was settled in London and Pattishall in Northhamptonshire, and no longer had any interest in the Tregeare properties. Degory, the second son, was fifty years old and had already been running the Tregeare farm for some time, where indeed he had lived all his life and there is no reason to suppose that his father's death caused any dramatic change in his lifestyle. Except of course that money was now beginning to flow, and the little Baron farming empire was expanding and changing.

In the Will of John Baron of Egloskerry who died in 1624 he left a property in South Tregeare to his nephew George, and another one to a Thomas Peers (or Pearce) whom he described as a kinsman, and there is also the messuage mentioned in the last chapter as having been bought in 1628 by John the son of the above John. To these three farms which were all in Baron possession must soon now be added the manor house, the property described on old documents and maps as Old Tregeare Mansion House, in which three generations of the Edgcombe family had been living since 1635. At some time round about 1740 this desirable residence, now one hundred and fifty years old, came into the possession of the Baron family and it may well be that some of the Baron money was used for this purpose.

Degory Baron died in 1738 being succeeded by his son Oliver who was twenty two years old and it is logical to suggest that he, like his father before him and his own children later on, was excited by the opportunities that the access to money were opening up before him. The acquisition of Old Tregeare would firmly establish them in the ranks of the gentry.

So we have a record of at least four properties in the Tregeare area which belonged to members of the Baron family or their close relatives – three farms, no doubt of varying sizes, and a mansion house. Within the scope of the information at present available it is difficult to establish who lived where, but there are several interesting possiblities.

Oliver Baron, (1716-1786) who was Degory's heir was actually his second son, his first son John having died in 1731 at the age of sixteen, and there is little doubt but that Oliver was the head of the family for it was his son Jasper who was credited later with the building of the present Tregeare House in 1790.

The other candidates, all of whom also stem from John and Joan Baron of Treludick (see page 52) include the following. Firstly the descendants of Jonathan Baron (1623-1702) and his wife Jane Moyse who had seven children, four sons and three daughters. The number of grandchildren is not known, nor are their names, but one daughter Margery married a Thomas Crocker and another, Joan, married a Peter Pryor. The eldest girl Catherine apparently died in 1714 a spinster, aged fifty seven.

Then there are the descendants of Ann Baron (1634-1684) who married William Stanburie, and also those of Sarah Baron (1626-1686) who married William Rowe in 1650. The Rowe family were obviously close to the Barons, and George Baron (1626-1686) was clearly very fond of his sister Sarah for in his Will his first legacy is to her, and the next one to her husband William. He also left generous sums of money to their five children, and appointed William Rowe a joint Executor of his Will. This friendly relationship between the two families obviously continued for there is a record that in the 18th century, eighty years later, a Mr Rowe bought the Manor of Laneast from the Arundell family, and that subsequently his son Roger held the manor in partnership with William Baron. The expansion continued.

Oliver Baron was married twice, firstly in 1752 to Joan Wilkinson who died in 1753, presumably in childbirth, though there is no evidence to support this. In 1762 he married again, to Elizabeth Booth who bore him six children in all and outlived him, dying in 1796.

This second half of the 18th century saw profound changes taking place in the story of the Barons of Tregeare. A few of those involved are listed above, but there could be more. This is the most interesting period in the story, and yet there would seem to be less concrete and reliable information about it than in the previous two hundred years. The Wills and sometimes the Inventories of many of these good people are available, but these are disappointing in the lack of information they contain, not only about the people involved but about the houses they lived in, and in these pre-photography days there are very few illustrations. By the middle of the 19th century, after a further and even more radical change, the flow of information begins again and we are able to get a clearer picture of both the houses and their occupants.

Portrait of a Gentleman,
probably Oliver Baron
1716 - 1786
(or is it William?)

Oliver Baron, as well as being a gentleman of means with an estate in Cornwall and property in London, had a successful career as a barrister of the Inner Temple and perforce had to spend much of his time in town. His children were Oliver William, born 1762, Ann born 1764, Elizabeth born 1766, Jasper born 1768, Frances Jane born 1770, and Marianne born 1772.

Oliver William, the eldest son and heir apparent, never married and in fact seems to have had little impact on Tregeare dying in 1793. Ann is an interesting character and a little mystery surrounds her adult life. Dorothy Lloyd and her brother, who did so much of the initial research into the history of the Barons of Tregeare, came across a reference to a marriage between Ann Baron and a Christopher Lethbridge of Launceston. Unfortunately the source of this report could not be relocated and it has never been confirmed, while the official Lethbridge records show that Christopher married a twenty six year old girl called Mary Copland in 1785. Mary bore him eight children and did not die until 1825, by which time Ann was sixty one years of age and presumably still a spinster, though this point cannot at present be verified. All we know for certain is that she was still a spinster in 1801, for there is an authentic record in the Public Record Office that at this date she was still living in the Old Tregeare Mansion House as Miss Ann Baron, paying a rent of £10 per annum.

Jasper Baron's Mother,
Elizabeth Booth

So it looks as though the report of Ann's marriage to Christopher is false. But there is a strange sequel to this story. Edward Galton Baron Lethbridge, who was a great-grandson of Christopher Lethbridge, and a subsequent owner of Tregeare in the early years of the present century, left an interesting diary which has proved to be an invaluable source of information, and also some further notes describing and commenting on the various Baron family portraits which at one time were to be found at Tregeare House. One of these portraits was of Ann Baron, and Mr. Lethbridge's note concerning it runs as follows –

"<u>Ann Baron</u>. Daughter of Oliver and Elizabeth Baron and sister of Jasper. Born 1764 August 11. Died on the eve of her wedding – her brocaded silk dress being in my possession and was worn at a fancy dress Ball by A.D.I.L. (Ada Dorothy Ivy Lethbridge, Edward Galton's wife.)"

What are we to make of this information? The notes give us no clue as to the date of the wedding – that – never – was. Could it have been in 1825 or later, when Ann and Christopher were both in their sixties? It could not have been pre-1785 for she was still alive in 1801. Or were they indeed old friends dating back to his bachelor days? Did Christopher visit her when she lived at Old Tregeare? Had she perhaps waited for him all those years? If so, to be thwarted on the eve of her wedding was particularly poignant. Or was she perhaps marrying someone else? And what was the cause of death? What a story that brocaded wedding dress could tell! There will be more to be said about Christopher Lethbridge in a later chapter, for he was quite a character.

Oliver and Elizabeth's next child was christened Elizabeth and was born in 1766. Very little is known about her, except that she and her sister Frances Jane, who was born in 1770, later left Cornwall to live in Suffolk and both died there c.1836. Neither of them married. Their younger sister Marianne also presents something of a mystery which has not yet been fully resolved. Again, we know practically nothing about her, but Edward Galton Lethbridge mentions her in his diary in April 1900. All he says that in clearing out a mass of old books and old deeds in the attic he came across "any amount of correspondence re a lunatick Miss Marianne Baron; actions at law; Estate labour and legal accounts etc, etc – nothing apparently of any value." It is difficult to say what this means, but it certainly looks as though Marianne was giving trouble in some way. Is this perhaps another skeleton in the cupboard!

Rec'd of Miss Ann Baron for half years Rent of Tregear Old Mansion house & Garden due D° 5 .. .. ..

— of William Saundercock for one Years Rent of two fields called East Town due D° 3 .. 5 .. ..

— of Thomas Pearn for one years Rent of Premises called Litcot due D° 40 .. .. ..

— of Ann Blewett for D° called Higher East Town due D° 1 .. 6 .. ..

— of Richard Bartlett for Ditto called Mill Park and Stabbages due Ditto 7 .. 8 .. 8

— of Ralph Venning for Ditto called Undertown due D° 1 .. 10 ..

— of M'rs Baron for half a Years Rent of Premises called Higher and Lower Hill Park Baker's Meadows & Orchard and Broomfield due D° 6 .. .. ..

— of George Bath for one Years Rent of his aforesaid Premises due Michas 1800 73 .. 10 .. ..

— of John Adams for Ditto D° 5 .. 1 .. ..

— of Ditto D° 1 .. 11 .. 6

— of Richard Rowe for Ditto D° 4 .. 4 .. ..

— of Peter Hodge for Ditto D° 1 .. 1 .. ..

— of Joseph Holman for Ditto D° 60 .. .. ..

— of Samuel Brown for Ditto D° 1 .. 2 .. ..

— of Richard Rowe for Ditto D° 21 .. .. ..

— of Miss Ann Baron for one Years rent due D° 10 .. .. ..

— of William Saundercock for one Years Rent due Michaelmas 1800 3 .. 5 ..

— of Thomas Pearn for Ditto D° 40 .. .. ..

— of Ann Blewett for Ditto D° 1 .. 6 ..

— of Richard Bartlett for Ditto D° 7 .. 8 .. 8

— of Ralph Venning for Ditto D° 1 .. 16 ..

— of M'rs Baron for Ditto D° 12 .. .. ..

A portion of the Tregeare Accounts for 1800. Note Miss Ann Baron. Courtesy of Public Record Office.

91

And so we come to Jasper Baron, in many ways the most important man in this story, for it is he who began the building of the magnificent west front of the present Tregeare House. Or perhaps it would be more prudent to say that it is he who was <u>credited</u> with the beginning of the building, and it is his name that appears in the large ornamental window that lights the stairwell and the inner hall.

Jasper was born in 1768 and the basic facts known about him are few. He is believed to have matriculated at Pembroke College, Oxford, and subsequently to have studied law in London. In 1794 he married Elizabeth Pearce of Mevagissey, and on the marriage certificate is described as "Jasper Baron, gent, of Stonehouse." Now, Stonehouse is in Devonport on the east bank of the Tamar River which divides Devon from Cornwall, and the manor of East Stonehouse belonged for centuries to the Edgcombe family. At present it is not known why Jasper had a residential qualification there, nor what his relationship was with the Edgcombes, and this is just another of the many unanswered questions about this generation of the Barons of Tregeare.

Edward Galton Lethbridge adds to the mystery by making the following comment in his Notes on the Family Portraits at Tregeare–

"The properties (i.e. the Tregeare Estate and the London Estate) had passed from Oliver (Barrister of the Inner Temple) who died May 20 1786 to his eldest child Oliver who died 1793 and left both to his mother (Elizabeth Booth whose portrait exists.) She died in 1796 and her fourth child Jasper succeeded. Query: since Jasper died 1798, was Tregeare built between 1796 and 1798, or begun earlier by his brother or mother?"

This is interesting information indeed for all previous records seem to point to "circa 1790" as the date of building. This date is given in the listing of Tregeare House as a Grade II building, the source of information quoted in this document being Pevsners "Buildings of England" 1970. Pevsner is of course a reliable witness and perhaps his use of the word "circa" can be stretched to include 1796 which is a much more logical date. In 1790 Jasper was only twenty two years old and was definitely not the owner of Tregeare. His elder brother was in possession at the time, and when he (Oliver William) died in 1793 he left the estates to his mother, as Edward Galton Lethbridge later reported. His mother, Elizabeth Booth as was, died in 1796 and it was then that Jasper inherited Tregeare and had the position and the resources to embark on a major building project. But should it have been his elder brother's name that was inscribed on the stairwell window?

This sequence of events was confirmed as true beyond doubt only a few years later, for in 1798 Jasper himself died, leaving all to his widow Elizabeth Pearce. Trustees were appointed to help her, but alas this arrangement did not work, the trustees found that the finances and administration of the estate were in some disarray and far too complicated for them to unravel. In the year 1800 they filed a suit with the Court of Chancery with a request that the Court should step in and advise, and matters passed temporarily out of their hands.

Concurrently with these financial and legal problems the health of the Barons of Tregeare was approaching a pathetic climax, for they were soon to disappear completely from the scene.

IN SUNDRY PLACES

Chapter 11 - Sadness and Wisdom

When Oliver Baron died in 1786 no one dreamt for a moment that within ten years he would be followed by his eldest son Oliver William (in 1793) and his widow Elizabeth Booth (in 1796), and then by his second son Jasper (in 1798). With four changes of ownership in such a short space of time, involving four Wills and four sets of legacies there is no wonder the family finances were put under severe stress. Many of the legacies were to be paid by a certain date, and interest was to accrue, usually at five percent. The complications were inevitably many and the resolving of all these problems became the responsibility of Jasper's widow Elizabeth Pearce the residual legatee and her two Trustees, Christopher Lethbridge, the Baron family solicitor, and John Pearce, brother of Elizabeth Pearce.

It could have been no surprise to anyone that this task was quite beyond the capabilities of the girl from Mevagissey, and within a few months it became apparent that it was also outside the scope of the Trustees. The principal trustee was no doubt Christopher Lethbridge who as family solicitor had drawn up Jasper's Will and no doubt also the Wills of Jasper's mother and brother. It is also possible that Christopher Lethbridge had earlier advised Oliver Baron, Jasper's father, for the firm of solicitors in Launceston, Lethbridge and Company, had been founded by Christopher in 1785, a year before Oliver died.

Jasper Baron's Will was a complicated affair, and the difficulty experienced in 1998 in obtaining a copy of it should have been a warning that all was not as straight forward as had been expected. The Cornish County Record Office supplied a copy which turned out to be not the original Will but a sizeable extract from it, the Public Record Office in Kew passed a request for a copy on to their Family Records Centre in London, who also supplied an extract from the Will – but not the same extract as the CRO – and ultimately it was necessary to employ a professional searcher who after two or three visits to Kew came up with a copy of the Will itself.

Its complications were immediately apparent and there were some curious differences between the original and the two extracts. The legal phraseology was in places almost impenetrable and there were two thousand words of it, including what amounted to a disclaimer on the part of the trustees, almost suggesting that they anticipated the trouble that was to follow. At this distance in time, now over two hundred years, and in view of the Court records which subsequently became available, these points are only of academic interest, but with hindsight it was a curious document to produce.

A short extract from the first part of the Will may be of interest. After a comment that he is leaving his sisters only twenty pounds each "as a token of the love and respect I bear them and who from the affluent circumstances they are in need not anything from me…." He says the following:-

> "all my freehold messuages lands tenements and hereditaments in the Parishes of Laneast and Tresmeer in the County of Cornwall aforesaid and all my estate therein in possession reversion or remainder whereof I have power to dispose I give devise and bequeath unto my dearly beloved wife Elizabeth Baron for and during the term of her natural life without impeachment of waste (wilful waste excepted) and from and immediately after the determination of that estate by forfeiture or otherwise in her lifetime then I give and devise the same premises unto my Brother in law John Pearce of Mevagissey in the said County of Cornwall Merchant and Christopher Lethbridge of Launceston in the County of Cornwall gentleman and their heirs during her life in trust…"

It is perhaps odd that in the above extract there is no mention of the Parish of Egloskerry in which he must have owned some land. Later in the Will he refers to his London estates, the old Manor of Paris Gardens, and directs his trustees to sell off such part of this estate as shall be necessary to pay all his debts and legacies etc., and to provide for the maintenance and education of his children.

One other rather strange phrase mentions the possibility of wilful waste by his wife and may suggest that he has fears in this direction. Was Elizabeth Pearce perhaps a spendthrift? If so then the provision of trustees is a very necessary safeguard, and it will be noted that the first one listed is her brother John Pearce, through it may possibly be modesty on the part of Christopher Lethbridge, who is drawing up the document, to put his own name second.

The first application by the Trustees to the Chancery Court was for a decision as to whether Jasper's Will was valid or not, and this was presumably born of the discovery that the legacies debts and expenses of the previous three owners of Tregeare – Oliver, Oliver William and Elizabeth Baron – had never been settled, so that Jasper's Will with a further set of requirements proved to be the last straw that broke the camel's back. The Court decree that the will was valid was issued on 18 February 1801, and a Master in Chancery was appointed by the Court to take an account and to appoint a receiver of the rents and profits.

With all due respect for the legal profession, without whose aid these days we may hardly exist, they made a meal of this case and they managed to drag it out for nearly nine years. It was not until 1809 that the Master made his report and matters were ultimately brought to a conclusion. The Court resumee of the case is typical of the age and of the profession, it is wordy in the extreme and is written in that exquisite legal jargon which is based on the conviction that no one is to be trusted and that one word should never be used when three will do. But it is thorough, and recites in detail the intricacies of the financial tangle into which these latter Barons had unwittingly become enmeshed. To anyone interested in their story and wishful of their welfare it makes fascinating reading, all twelve thousand words of it.

The cost to the family of this nine year long debate can perhaps be imagined, and at times it almost seemed that the original intention of the case had been relegated to second place while learned counsel for the plaintiffs and for the defendants argued points of law. The story they unfolded is at once interesting, logical and pathetic. It is the story of a family of yeoman farmers, the backbone of the Cornish as well as the English nation, who by dint of hard work and honest husbandry worked their way upwards in their world until they were legitimately able to call themselves gentlemen. Their struggle was given a tremendous boost when one of them turned out to be a business genius and found his way into Aladdin's cave and great wealth, and having no children of his own, left a large sum of money for the benefit of future generations of his nephews and nieces.

Whether George Baron's generosity and altruism was a good thing for the family in the long run it is hard to say, but he has to be remembered with affection if only for the fact that it was his money that ultimately made the building of the present Tregeare House possible, and for this little architectural gem we must be thankful.

Extract from the long Court Report. Courtesy of Public Record Office.

The Chancery Court, having decided that Jasper's Will was indeed valid began their investigation into its complexities and soon found that it was necessary to go back at least twenty years to find the source of the trouble. They interrogated Elizabeth Pearce, Jasper's widow and from her they must have discovered the true extent of the muddle.

Jasper's father Oliver in his Will dated 28 May 1782 left a legacy of six hundred pounds to each of five of his children. He excluded his eldest son, Oliver William, as he was his heir in law and would ultimately inherit the estate, but he included his second son Jasper together with his four daughters. Three years later, in 1785, he revoked the legacy to Jasper and in its place devised to him all his freehold and leasehold properties "in or near the parishes of Laneast, Tresmeer, Boyton, Lezant and elsewhere in the County of Cornwall." At this time Jasper would be seventeen years old. There was only one incumbrance on this bequest, that of a mortgage of one thousand pounds made with a Mrs Margaret Davey in 1784, this being a charge on the Laneast portion of the estate.

Before he died Oliver seems to have revoked the Codicil, or his Will, for the Master in Chancery who had to take the decision declared that to all intents and purposes he died intestate, and there was in fact sufficient doubt as to Oliver's ultimate intentions as to enable learned Counsel to argue for both the Plaintiffs (John Pearce and Christopher Lethbridge) and the Defendants (Elizabeth Baron, widow, and her children Ann, Elizabeth, Frances Jane and Marianne). The basic four legacies amounted to two thousand, four hundred pounds, and on Oliver's death the cash to satisfy these was simply not available, so the responsibility for the debt devolved on Oliver William his heir. Oliver William himself died in 1793 before all the provisions of his father's Will had been carried out, and he left all to his mother (Elizabeth Booth).

Poor Elizabeth Booth; she found herself facing an almost impossible task. Presumably she knew that her husband had borrowed two thousand pounds in 1768 though some of this may have been paid back. But she was faced with the fact that she had insufficient working capital, and so she borrowed, one thousand pounds from John Elliott at four and a half percent p.a., five hundred pounds from Elizabeth Kingdom, spinster, at five percent, five hundred pounds from Montague Booth at five percent and five hundred pounds from Mary Booth, spinster, also at five percent.

Elizabeth died in 1796, and her Will demonstrated that she obviously had still not grasped the fact that sooner or later some of the properties she owned would have to be sold to pay off all these various debts. There were indeed three quite distinct properties involved, firstly the Cornish estates centred on Laneast and Egloskerry parishes, secondly the principal money spinner the Paris Garden Estates in the Parish of Christ Church, Surrey, and thirdly a small estate consisting of a house, garden and land in the Parish of St George the Martyr, Mitcham, part of which was freehold and part copyhold.

In her Will Elizabeth (Booth) Baron left all her freehold lands to her son Jasper, and legacies of five hundred pounds to Elizabeth Booth, eight hundred pounds to Jane Booth, and to her four daughters Ann Baron, Elizabeth Baron, Frances Jane Baron, and Marianne Baron four thousand, five hundred pounds a piece, payable two years after her death. In the meantime interest was to be paid at five percent. What her thoughts were on where all this money was coming from are not recorded, but presumably she discussed them with Jasper, who was left carrying the baby. He subsequently discovered that as security for the money she borrowed she had pledged her children's inheritance.

It seems a pity to have had to apply to the Courts for help in sorting out the mess, but Christopher Lethbridge knew what he was doing and the balance was ultimately restored. One of the first decisions taken by the Master examining the cause was to appoint Christopher Lethbridge the Receiver of Rents and Profits, and this put him in a very powerful position indeed, for the next decision taken was to authorise him to pay the Defendant Ann Baron two thousand pounds on account of the four thousand, five hundred pound legacy left her by her mother, though first he was to pay his own account of two thousand pounds plus expenses, and to settle the costs incurred by the other Defendants.

Why Ann Baron was singled out for this preferential treatment is not stated, but she had a very powerful advocate in Christopher Lethbridge, and with hindsight and the knowledge that she died on the eve of her wedding it is possible to create all sorts of scenarios. She was at this time living in the Old Tregeare Mansion House, the life of a lady of leisure. She was thirty nine years old. Christopher was forty three and at the height of his very successful career. He was playing a leading role in the public life of Launceston in which ancient town he filled many important offices including that of Mayor and Town Clerk, and at one time he was under Sheriff of Cornwall. He had been married for eighteen years and had eight surviving children ranging in age from five to eighteen years. He was in fact an eminently respectable and successful man but it would have been interesting on occasion to have been a fly on the wall at Old Tregeare.

When the Court case finally came to an end in 1809 the Baron fortunes had been dented but by no means broken, though Jasper's widow Elizabeth Pearce must have been a sadder and wiser woman. Of her two children William was twelve years old and Elizabeth Ann was ten and their health was giving her some concern. A portrait had been painted of them together, showing them to be a charming pair, but their lives were not destined to be full and happy for they both died at a comparatively young age, and they were indeed the last of this particular line of Barons.

IN SUNDRY PLACES

Chapter 12 - The Transition

When the 18th Century came to an end the situation facing Jasper's widow, Elizabeth Pearce, was not a particularly happy one. Left without a husband to support and console her and to carry the responsibility of managing the estate, and with two small children to rear, she must have felt at times that life was not dealing fairly with her. Many people may have envied her position as mistress of many broad acres, with an additional income from her London estates, but without the cash to settle the many debts and legacies she had also inherited her life was not without its anxieties. Indeed her cash flow problems must have seemed insuperable.

Inevitably she was forced to rely more and more on the trustees Jasper had appointed, namely her brother John Pearce, and the family solicitor Christopher Lethbridge. How friendly her relationship was with John and Christopher is not known but it may well be that it was amicable and that when the trustees decided they had to appeal to the Court for help that the division between Plaintiff and Defendant was simply necessary to conform to legal requirements.

Elizabeth was probably much more concerned about the health and well being of her children than she was about the unfolding legal situation, but unfortunately medical information about individual families of this period is practically non-existent. With hindsight it is possible to hazard guesses but they are definitely only guesses and it is all too easy to jump to the wrong conclusion.

One fact that seems to be reliable is that Jasper and Elizabeth actually had three children, though only two of the these survived infancy. In the Cornish archives two pedigrees of the Baron family have survived, one written in the 18th century and one in the 19th. These indicate that Jasper's first born was a girl whom they named Elizabeth, but who died in infancy. This girl was probably born in 1794 or 1795 and was followed by William who was born in 1796. Unfortunately it is not possible to say if there was anything wrong with the child or its birth, or whether there was some weakness inherent in its mother.

William, who was born in 1796, appears to have been a normal boy. When he was about ten years old his portrait was painted together with his sister Elizabeth Ann by Samuel Woodforde R.A. and this shows them to be a good-looking, chubby faced pair, and healthy. This portrait, together with one of Jasper their father is now in the possession of Mr Richard Lethbridge who with his brother Christopher was happily able to purchase several family portraits which were being sold off by open auction in 1981. An account of these portraits is given later (See Appendix A).

William inherited the Tregeare Estates in August 1812 on the death of his mother. He was sixteen years old at the time and he must have felt a little bewildered by the responsibilities suddenly thrust upon him. Inevitably he too would have had to rely on the wisdom of Christopher Lethbridge who had been appointed by the Court as the Receiver of Rents and Profits, and was in effect in the driving seat.

In 1825 William was appointed Sheriff of Cornwall, which was a great honour for a young man, and he was also a local Magistrate. His term of office as Sheriff was not without incident, and though details are not known there was a rumour of some irregularity with regard to public money.

In 1826 he fell in love with Elizabeth King the younger daughter of Philip Gidley King, Governor of New South Wales in Australia, and wished to marry her, but for some reason this never came to pass, and at the present time the mystery remains. Harriet Lethbridge, youngest daughter of Christopher Lethbridge was a close personal friend of Elizabeth King's and she refers to this romance in a letter to her husband –

> "The flirtation I alluded to is between Elizabeth and Mr Baron; we spent a few days at Tregeare, and on our return, Mr B. followed, and has been staying at Madford ever since; To you I may own, he has spoken to me he has told me his wishes, and enquired if E. was perfectly disengaged as if not, he could not stay longer in Lanson (Launceston). I assured him she was, and he begged I would not name it to anyone, but he should continue here and endeavour to ascertain whether his attentions are agreeable to her. I have put E. on her guard, as it is now evident to everyone, what he means as yet, I can hardly tell, whether E. means to encourage him or not, she has expressed to me, that she could be very happy in the country and that Mr B. is not disagreeable to her, but there is one objection, and I think only one, which if she can disregard it, she will do well to accept such an offer."

Jasper Baron of Tregeare 1768 – 1798

Elizabeth Ann, the last Baron of Tregeare

Elizabeth Ann Baron

Jasper's Children,
William and Elizabeth Ann

103

Harriet goes on to say that Elizabeth's mother, Mrs Anna Josepha King had not as yet expressed her opinion either one way or the other, but it has been suggested by others that it was indeed Mrs King who put an end to the romance. What the 'objection' was is not stated. Did William have a 'problem'? Whatever it was, Harriet reported that her father and her sisters Mary and Rebecca used to joke about it.

This letter from Harriet to her husband Phillip Parker King, who was at sea at the time, was written in 1826, immediately before her own departure from Plymouth to Australia with four of her children. The letter also demonstrates how close a relationship already existed between the Lethbridge and King families and the Barons of Tregeare.

William was not destined to live very much longer for he died in March 1827, and even his death is accompanied by a tantalising conflict of information. Edward Galton Baron Lethbridge, writing c.1900, says

"William died (intestate) of fever after a brief illness..."

but the Cornwall Gazette published the following fulsome obituary–

"On Monday last, at Madford, the residence of John King Lethbridge Esq. of Launceston, William Baron Esq. of Tregeare House, in this County, universally esteemed by his numerous friends for the amiability of his character, the urbanity of his manners, the kindness of his heart, and the genuineness of his professions. Of this deservedly lamented Gentleman, it may without ostentation be said, that in him, the County has sustained the loss of one of its esteemed Magistrates; his family the most affectionate of relatives, his domestics, the kindness (sic) of Masters, and the Poor, a steady and liberal benefactor in their distresses. – He died at the early age of twenty nine, and bore his long protracted illness with christian fortitude and pious resignation to the dispensation of the divine will, breathing his last without even a sigh."

If the Cornish Gazette is right and William suffered a long and protracted illness it suggests that he may possibly have been a consumptive, for tuberculosis was the great killer disease of the period. Actually, he may well have experienced a fever towards the end – he may have caught a cold – so that perhaps both reports are true. It is interesting that he died at Madford, in Launceston, and not in his own house. Could he still have been chasing Elizabeth King who was a frequent visitor at Madford?

According to all accounts Elizabeth Ann Baron grew up to be an intelligent and charming woman, and Millicent Lethbridge, who later wrote a fascinating account of her own family history and their connection with Tregeare, said she must have been singularly lovely and intellectual. She had many friends of similar age and social station in the Launceston area, notably from the six daughters of Christopher and Mary Lethbridge at Madford who were noted for their good looks, and also Mary and Elizabeth King. Mary King married Robert Copland Lethbridge and her brother Phillip married Harriet, the youngest of the six Lethbridge girls. Elizabeth King's romance with William never came to anything but she was an active member of the social circle and she has been remembered, not only for her looks and vivacity, but also for her singing voice which was exceptionally pure and which in those pre-radio and television days was a social asset of great value.

Elizabeth Ann Baron was a little younger than the other members of her set and was perhaps not as active as the rest, for alas, her health was never good, and though no doubt she experienced moments of happiness these were fleeting and her adult life generally was burdened with sadness. When she was eighteen she was courted by Christopher Lethbridge's eldest son John King who was thirty, and they were married by licence in 1819. She bore him two sons in quick succession but both babies died in infancy and left her further debilitated. In July 1826 John's sister Harriet wrote to her husband

> "Mrs John is very weak and ill, she appears not to have derived any benefit from her journey to Bath, but is rather worse."

and in September she followed this up with –

> "Mrs John continues weak and poorly, nor do I expect she will ever be better."

Elizabeth Ann lived for another seven years but on the first of February 1833 she gave up the struggle and died and was buried in the Baron family vault underneath the Chancel in Egloskerry church. She was the last of the Barons of Tregeare and her death brought to an end the long story of a farming family that over the centuries had the built up a little local empire, until at the beginning of the 18th century the

Christopher Lethbridge of Madford
1760 - 1830

Mary (Polly) Copland, his wife

J. C. Baron Lethbridge
1839 - 1885

Millicent Galton Bunbury, his wife

acquisition of wealth had altered their lives and transported them into the 'gentry' class. There are signs that over the years health was sometimes a problem, several children died when very young or in their infancy, and towards the end thirty years of age was beginning to look like a magic figure to be achieved.

Memorial Tablet to Elizabeth Ann Lethbridge
(nee Baron) in Egloskerry Church

Family portraits of many of the Barons survived in Tregeare House and helped to keep their memory alive, until in 1981 the whole contents of the house were sold to the highest bidder, and in some cases to the most remote stranger. With this sale a vital historical link was broken, and Tregeare House is the poorer for the loss of some of its treasures. It is hoped that the few scraps of the story that have been hereby picked up will do something towards reminding the reader about this fascinating family.

Scraps of information about the Barons keep popping up from time to time, rather like pieces of a long lost jigsaw puzzle, and occasionally some of them fit. One such item concerns Marianne Baron, Jasper's youngest sister who was born in 1772. You may remember that on page eighty seven Edward Lethbridge in his diary reported finding some old correspondence concerning "a lunatick Marianne Baron". Very little is known about Marianne but it now transpires that in 1823 she married the Rev. W.B.Fennell who was the Rector of Compton Valence in Dorset. She would have been fifty one at the time and hence is hardly likely to have been "lunatick" in the sense of madness. Perhaps she was just a little high spirited when young.

Now, what about the house that Jasper built? After all, the whole object of this present exercise was to find out about the origins of the present Tregeare House, and about the farmhouse that previously occupied the site. So it is with particular regret that it has to be reported that in all the research that has been carried out over the last two years only one fairly casual reference to it has been found. This occurs in some notes Edward Lethbridge made c.1900 about the family portraits that were in his possession. In referring to Jasper's portrait he wrote –

> "He added the main block of the mansion to existing premises about 1790 the builder being the father of old William Burt of Lanson (who often worked for me)"

At first sight it would seem impossible that anyone could build a mansion of the size and beauty of Tregeare and leave no written record of it, and having been baffled by the absence of information in the Cornish County Record Office this opinion was voiced to one of their archivists. His reply was that sad and impractical as this might seem it was by no means untypical. Of course there would have been written records at one time but for some reason, or rather for a variety of reasons, these have obviously not been preserved. It is not unusual in fact to find that some small and insignificant cottage is documented up to the hilt, and yet a large and important house such as Tregeare has left no record in the archives. And with this we must be content.

IN SUNDRY PLACES

Chapter 13 - Enter the Lethbridges

The Lethbridges can boast a very distinguished pedigree and can trace their line back to Danish invaders before the Norman Conquest. The name has suffered many changes in its passages through the centuries, and it has been said that it originated as 'Leather Breeches'. The family has been active in the West Country from a very early date, and powerful branches were established in Somerset, Devon and Cornwall, the last two having their centres in Okehampton and Launceston respectively. Both these latter two became ultimately connected with the development of Australia from its founding in the last years of the 18th century, and there is no doubt that the Australian branch of the Lethbridge family has made, and is still making, a significant contribution to the development and prosperity of that great country.

A glance at the Lethbridge Family Tree No.1 will show how the Launceston branch of the family came about and it lists several members who have had a very positive influence on the Tregeare story. Most prominent amongst these is Christopher Lethbridge (1760-1830) who has already been mentioned in this account (see page 89). In his public life he was a figure of immense respectability, and as family solicitors to the Barons, and of course the Lethbridges, he exercised great influence and was responsible for taking many important decisions. He built up an extremely flourishing firm of solicitors in Launceston which is still in being today though its name has suffered several changes since 1785.

Christopher lived in a big house in Madford Lane in Launceston, in a commanding position and with a large garden. Photographs of Madford House are displayed in the Lawrence House Museum in Launceston but it has long since disappeared and on its site were built the Inland Revenue office and the Public Library.

His private life is perhaps not quite so open to scrutiny and it would seem that he had an eye for the ladies, but his marriage to Mary Copland lasted for forty years until her death in 1825. Mary, who was apparently known as Polly was a strong character too, with progressive religious views which persuaded her to become a Methodist. Her marriage to Christopher could not have been too

Lethbridge Family Tree No. 1

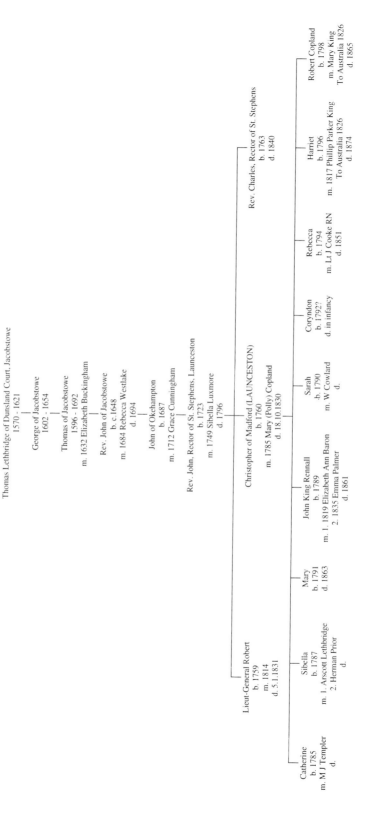

Thomas Lethbridge of Dunsland Court, Jacobstowe
1570 - 1621

George of Jacobstowe
1602 - 1654

Thomas of Jacobstowe
1596 - 1692
m. 1632 Elizabeth Buckingham

Rev. John of Jacobstowe
b. c.1648
m. 1684 Rebecca Westlake
d. 1694

John of Okehampton
b. 1687
m. 1712 Grace Cunningham

Rev. John, Rector of St. Stephens, Launceston
b. 1723
m. 1749 Sibella Luxmore
d. 1796

Christopher of Madford (LAUNCESTON)
b. 1760
m. 1785 Mary (Polly) Copland
d. 18.10.1830

Rev. Charles, Rector of St. Stephens
b. 1763
d. 1840

Lieut-General Robert
b. 1759
m. 1814
d. 5.1.1831

Catherine
b. 1785
m. M J Templer
d.

Sibella
b. 1787
m. 1. Arscott Lethbridge
2. Herman Prior
d.

John King Rennall
b. 1789
m. 1. 1819 Elizabeth Ann Baron
2. 1835 Emma Palmer
d. 1861

Sarah
b. 1790
m. W Cowlard
d.

Mary
b. 1791
d. 1863

Coryndon
b. 1792?
d. in infancy

Rebecca
b. 1794
m. Lt J Cooke RN
d. 1851

Harriet
b. 1796
m. 1817 Phillip Parker King
To Australia 1826
d. 1874

Robert Copland
b. 1798
m. Mary King
To Australia 1826
d. 1865

unhappy, for during the restoration of the grounds of Tregeare House recently, and the clearance of the undergrowth, a granite seat was discovered. On the seat are carved the initials C. and M.L. and the date 1810 which was the year of their Silver Wedding anniversary. It is possible that this slab of granite was intended originally as the lintel of a doorway for it is very finely carved and in a very good state of preservation after nearly two hundred years, the best part of which was probably spent in the shrubbery. If its intention was to mark twenty five years of happily married life it has obviously succeeded.

After Mary's death it is possible that Christopher's eye began to rove again. His friendship with Ann Baron has been mentioned and it

The granite record of Christopher Lethbridge's Silver Wedding

would seem that there were perhaps others. His daughter Harriet, who emigrated to Australia in 1826 left her second son John living at Madford under the care of her father and her two sisters Mary and Rebecca. But she was not happy about it and expressed her fears in letters to her husband who was at sea –

> "I am very anxious about our poor John. Rebecca writes me, in case my Father marries (which God forbid) she intends going to her cottage and taking Mary and John with her; I have written to your Mother (Mrs Gidley King) to say I never can agree to that woman having charge of him…"

"That woman's" name was Pauline, and in another letter about her Father Harriet says –

> "I do not know what to think of his conduct in a certain quarter,

sometimes I fear the worst, at others think he must see how obnoxious she is to the whole party…"

These fears are perfectly legitimate and normal in a mother, but life has a habit of going on whether we like it or not, and solves its own problems in the fullness of time. There is no record of Christopher having married Pauline, nor of any intention to marry Ann Baron, and he ultimately died in 1830 which put an end to the problem.

The plaque on No. 5 Southgate Street, Launceston

IN THIS HOUSE WAS BORN
Cᴬᴾᵀ PHILIP GIDLEY KING, R.N.
(1758 – 1808).
GOVERNOR OF
NEW SOUTH WALES,
1800–1806.
THE CITY OF LAUNCESTON,
TASMANIA,
FOUNDED IN 1806,
WAS NAMED IN HONOUR
OF HIS BIRTHPLACE.

One matter remains unrecorded, and that is Christopher's friendship with Philip Gidley King. Like Christopher, Philip was a Launceston boy and their friendship began at an early age. Their paths diverged as they grew up and Philip Gidley King's career blossomed when, as a Naval officer, he went to Australia with the first fleet of convict ships in 1788. He subsequently became an illustrious Governor of New South Wales, and is possibly Launceston's most famous son, and as two of his four children married Lethbridges (and a third one nearly so) no apology is really necessary for including a brief account of his life, and this can be found in Appendix B on page 186.

When Christopher Lethbridge's first son was born, Philip Gidley King became his godfather and the boy was christened John King Rennall Lethbridge. He followed his father into the legal profession and became a partner in the firm of Lethbridge and Co. in 1812 at the age of twenty three. He was well known in the area and played a significant role in the history of Tregeare by uniting the Baron and Lethbridge families and injecting into the Tregeare Estates new vigour. This will be dealt with in a later chapter, but first several other of Christopher Lethbridge's ten children are worthy of attention, for although they are not in the direct line of ownership of Tregeare they are nonetheless an essential part of the rich tapestry that constitutes the Lethbridge story. And all have an individual contribution to make.

Christopher's first born was Catherine, born in 1785. She married a Captain James Templer and bore him several children, one boy at least being christened Frederic Octavius Lethbridge, and one wonders whether this implies that he was the eighth child. Catherine's younger sister Harriet in writing to her husband Phillip Parker King who was at sea, rather curiously always refers to her sister as 'Mrs Templer'

113

and not by her Christian name. Perhaps it is wrong to read too much into this apparent formality between sisters but the impression given is that Harriet did not entirely approve of her elder sister. One of Catherine's children Hebe, married a John Venn Prior and had children. She is reported to have repeated to her children this strange little verse –

> "If Lethbridge were asked which to him was most dear,
> A reform loving Prince or reform hating peer,
> The answer would quick to our memory bring,
> To pay court to a Baron, he deserted a King."

No explanation of these odd lines has been found but it is fairly easy to make a shrewd guess as to their meaning. John King Lethbridge of course paid court to Elizabeth Ann Baron, and married her. Could it have been that a previous love of his was Elizabeth King, the third daughter of Philip Gidley King? If so it adds point to the concern that William Baron had in approaching Elizabeth King, and about which he spoke to Harriet Lethbridge who was Elizabeth's friend. (See page 101). It is possible to identify the reform loving prince as the Prince Regent but the reform hating peer is more difficult. Drawing a bow at a venture could it have been Lord Sidmouth who is known to have been involved in the reforms that the Prince Regent was pushing in the House of Lords?

Catherine had five sisters in all, or indeed six if one counts the last born, Elizabeth, who died in infancy. Sibella was born in 1787, two years younger than Catherine and appears to have had a highly strung emotional nature. At her brother's wedding reception Harriet reported that "poor Belle went off into hysterics." She was also very upset when this brother Robert Copland and her sister Harriet both decided to emigrate to Australia. Belle's married life was also not very stable. She married first a cousin John Arscott Lethbridge, but this did not last, and she later married Herman Prior. This also apparently came to grief for Prior is reported as having a second wife in Elizabeth King, Harriet's youngest daughter. If Herman Prior was related to James Prior who married Catherine's daughter Hebe the family relationship becomes even more complicated.

Catherine's second sister Mary was the only one not to marry. She was born in 1791 and lived all her life at Madford, dying at the age of seventy five. Next comes Sarah, born in 1790 who married a W. Cowlard. The Lethbridge and Cowlard families became very closely related through marriage and through work. In 1834 John Lethbridge

Cowlard became a partner in the firm of solicitors founded by Christopher, and by 1874 it became known as Cowlard and Cowlard.

Rebecca Lethbridge married Lieutenant John Cooke RN, whose ship was HMS Adventure, and she lived at Madford while her husband was at sea. And this brings us to Harriet the last surviving daughter of Christopher Lethbridge, and the most remarkable. She and her brother Robert Copland, together with four of her children sailed to Australia in 1826, determined to make new lives for themselves in this exciting and developing country, and in so doing they opened up an entirely new and absorbing chapter in the history of the Lethbridge family. They never forgot their Cornish background and to this day their affection for this part of Cornwall has remained an important link between the Old Country and the New.

Christopher Lethbridge died in 1830 full of years and job satisfaction. He was seventy years old and could look back on a life crowded with incident; he had founded a highly successful firm of solicitors in Launceston, and though this pond may be considered a fairly small one he was a fish of some size. In his public life he had been Town Clerk and at one time Mayor of Launceston, and was regarded by many as a figure of great respectability and one of the town's most influential residents. As a lawyer and the family solicitor of the Barons he had steered them through their last great economic storm, and had cleverly engaged a Master in Chancery as a pilot when the going got a bit rough. He emerged from this storm as the undisputed Captain of the ship, with the Court solidly endorsing his navigation.

His private life turned out to be more successful than he could have hoped for. His marriage lasted for than forty years, and the fact that he was able to commemorate the first twenty five years of these by carving his and his wife's initials on a block of granite suggests that it was reasonably stable. This block of granite is a mute record of the occasion and a reminder to all of us that to be blest with a stable marriage is a blessing indeed.

The marriage produced nine children, eight of whom survived into adulthood, and his two sons ensured the continuation of his line, not only in this country but also on the other side of the world in Australia. Both branches developed vigorous shoots, prospering and expanding and making their mark in a variety of professions and callings. Christopher Lethbridge was indeed the founder of two large families, both of which are flourishing today and both of which still have an affectionate regard for North Cornwall and the Launceston area, and even more particularly for Tregeare.

When he died his death was noticed by the Royal Cornwall Gazette of 23rd October 1830 who printed the following short, and perhaps slightly wayward, obituary.

*"At Launceston on Friday the 5th inst,
Christopher Lethbridge Esq., aged 73,
many years deputy Recorder of that Town,
a man universally esteemed for his urbanity of manners,
strict adherence to business, and attention to the wants of
all around him; his loss will be severely felt by a large
Circle of Friends, and the government and management of
the Town will have to deplore the loss of an attentive officer."*

IN SUNDRY PLACES

Chapter 14 - A New World

At first sight the link between Tregeare House and the Lethbridge and King families, both in this country and in Australia, may seem a fairly tenuous one, but it has survived the test of time and nearly two hundred years of change, during which the ownership of Tregeare has passed into other hands. But the bond of affection is still there, and as we reach the Millenium celebrations it can be said to be as strong, and maybe even stronger, than ever.

When Philip Gidley King settled in Australia and became Governor of New South Wales he called his family farm 'Denheved', which is the ancient name for Launceston, his birthplace. And when his daughter Mary married Robert Copland Lethbridge and also settled in Australia they built themselves a home which they named 'Werrington', again as a reminder of this part of Cornwall which was their homeland. And John King, the second son of Robert and Mary called his home 'Tregeare'.

Governor King had four children and his eldest son Phillip Parker also married a Lethbridge, Harriet the sister of Robert Copland, so that the ties between the two families were inevitably very close. Phillip Parker King, like his father, went into the Royal Navy, and had a very distinguished career, ultimately achieving the rank of Admiral. He excelled as a hydrographer and was responsible for much of the original surveying of the northern coasts of Australia and the southern coasts of South America. When, at the age of twenty eight, he decided it was time to take a wife his mother suggested he should visit Cornwall again to see her old friend Mrs Christopher Lethbridge, who had a family of beautiful daughters.

Phillip did just this, and indeed found himself a wife hereby. He knew parts of Cornwall well, having spent his school holidays there as a boy, and he fell in love with Harriet Lethbridge at first sight.. He was introduced to her one Sunday morning outside the church of St. Mary Magdalene in Launceston and her mother invited him to dinner after the service. The romance progressed rapidly, and on 29th January 1817 they were married. About eight years later their miniatures were painted and showed them to be an extremely handsome couple.

Harriet King (nee Lethbridge)   *Phillip Parker King*

At this time Phillip was at the height of his career and was elected a fellow of the Royal Society and the Royal Linnean Society.

Philip Gidley King's second child was a daughter Anna Maria, born in 1793. She was educated in England, being at school in Greenwich, and when she was nineteen married Hannibal Hawkins MacArthur and spent the rest of her life in Australia. Hannibal's younger brother Lieutenant Charles MacArthur R.N. was due to travel out with Harriet and her party, and was actually commissioned to make all the arrangements for the voyage, as well as to buy a small flock of sheep to take with them.

In this he was something less than successful. After travelling to Europe in search of sheep he finally bought some in Sussex, but on reaching Australia they were found to be of inferior quality to those they already had, and were sold at a loss. He also fell out with the Captain of the ship they were proposing to travel in and cancelled the booking. He found another ship, the 'Cumberland' but managed to quarrel with her skipper too, to the extent that they ultimately sailed without him as he was not to be found when the time came. One version of this sorry story is that the Captain refused to take him, but whatever the truth he was left behind although all his luggage was aboard.

The third daughter of Philip Gidley King, Elizabeth, has already been mentioned for it was she who at one time was flirting with William Baron, and could possibly have been the subject of the little poem quoted on page 119. Elizabeth ultimately married a widower, Charles Runciman, who was an artist, and died childless.

Governor King's youngest daughter Mary married Harriet's brother Robert Copland Lethbridge in July 1826, and within three weeks was off to Australia to begin her new life there. John King Rennall Lethbridge gave them twenty five pounds as a wedding present and in a speech at the Wedding Breakfast said he hoped that when they had been married as long as he had (actually seven years) he hoped they would be as reluctant to be unmarried as he was. Toasts were drunk to Phillip Parker King who was at sea and could not be present, and apart from his absence it was a very friendly and happy occasion.

Robert Copland Lethbridge of Forest Vale

Before leaving for Australia Harriet records that they all spent a few days at Tregeare as the guests of William Baron, and this must have been in the nature of an official farewell to the house that they all knew well and of which they must have hoped that Elizabeth King would one day be the mistress. Elizabeth was probably in the party at this visit, and also her mother, together with Harriet and her children, and Robert Copland and Mary. They could not possibly have guessed at this time that within a year William Baron who was only twenty nine years old would be dead, and that Tregeare House and Estate would become the property of his sister Elizabeth Ann and her husband John King Rennall Lethbridge.

From Tregeare they moved on to Madford House in Launceston, and very soon it was time for their departure from Plymouth in the good ship 'Cumberland'. The emigration party included Harriet with four of her sons, Essington, Robert, Charles and Frederick. Her husband Philip had recently left England in HMS Adventure for South American waters, taking with him their eight year old son Philip, and their second son John was being left in Launceston, where he was at school, and was to live with his grandfather at Madford. Also in the party were Harriet's brother Robert Copland and his bride Mary, the youngest daughter of Governor King.

To add to Harriet's responsibilities she was also pregnant and expecting to be confined before the ship reached Australia, so she had taken the precaution of engaging a mid-wife to sail with them since there was no doctor aboard the ship. This sounds quite a formidable outlook for a young married woman with four children, the eldest of whom was barely six years old, and indeed it was, for it would seem that she was the leader of the whole party, the rock on whom everyone else depended.

But then, Harriet was a quite extraordinary young woman, married at twenty one and now only thirty she was not only shepherding and mothering this gathering in a very hazardous and tedious voyage, but on arrival in Australia she was proposing to take over control of Dunheved the family farm which had been under management while they had been in England during the last three years.

The 'Cumberland' left Plymouth on the nineteenth of September 1826 and Harriet's party were seen off by Mrs King, Elizabeth, Mary Lethbridge and Johnny, Harriet's son, and Major General Robert Lethbridge who was Harriet's Uncle. Harriet wrote regularly to her husband keeping him informed of what was going on though she never knew when, or if, he was going to receive her letters. But passing ships were used as post boxes and it was surprising how many of them arrived safely, if sometimes after several months. The very act of writing them must have been a comfort to her for at least she was able to share her problems and anxieties. Fortunately for us many of these letters survived and came into the possession of Dorothy Walsh, Harriet King's great-granddaughter who transcribed, edited and published them in a splendid book under the title of 'The Admiral's Wife'. This book is a revelation as the letters disclose the trials and tribulations of the time, the long and tedious voyage to the other side of the world, the privations that had to be endured, and the astonishing fortitude and strength of character of this young woman.

Harriet must have had an iron constitution for there are no complaints in her letters about her health, but her brother Robert Copland was not so lucky. He was a kind and affectionate young man and Harriet records her appreciation of the support he gave to her, but he suffered from a nervous disability and found the heat of the Australian winter very trying. By profession he was a lawyer, but his intention was to abandon law for the farm, though on arrival in Australia it was suggested to him that a sudden switch to farming might be too much for him and that also the income practising law for a year or two would be of very great value until they were firmly established.

In 1849 Robert Copland was reported to be in good health and spirits and planning to expand his farm. Mary and he had seven children in all, five sons and two daughters from whom have sprung many well-known Australian families. Their eldest, Christopher, was in fact the only one to die childless, but the others were all blest with numerous offspring. The second son, John King, became a J.P., a coroner and returning officer. Originally of Dunheved the family farm he later built his own home which he called Tregeare. His brother Robert Copland who was born in 1838 at Werrington also became a Justice of the Peace and lived at 'Forest Vale'. His photographs show him to have been a fine figure of a man. Robert and Mary's youngest child, Elizabeth Margaret, married her cousin Arthur Septimus King, Harriet King's seventh and last son who was born in 1827 soon after his mother's arrival in Australia.

From the family tree of the Tregeare branch it can be seen that this stem of the family is extremely fruitful and flourishing, Robert Copland and Mary's five sons and two daughters, producing in the first generation of children twenty seven sons and twenty daughters. Their close relations the King's, headed by Phillip Parker and Harriet were likewise the progenitors of no fewer than thirty four sons and twenty one daughters. In addition, Phillip Parker's sister Anna Maria gave birth to five sons and six daughters.

Another branch of the Lethbridge family also had its origins in Tregeare in John King Rennall's younger son who was called John King after his father. This second John King was born in 1848, became a clergyman, and in 1870 became Vicar of Laneast. He married Olympe Chapuis, a Swiss orphan who had been adopted some years before as a companion of the young Millicent Bunbury who later married John Christopher Baron. A son, Edwin Arscott was born in 1875 who married Irene Heppingstone and they also emigrated and settled in Western Australia.

The Tregeare branch descendants enumerated above are not the only Lethbridges in Australia by any manner of means, and other branches stem from Lieut-Colonel Christopher Lethbridge of the Madras Army and Captain Robert Lethbridge RN, both of whom were the sons of Christopher Lethbridge of Okehampton in Devon. This tremendous tally represents a record of which any family could justly feel proud, especially as all the early settlers suffered great hardship in those far off days, not only on the long and dangerous voyage out from the mother country, but in taming a savage and undeveloped country and helping to establish a great nation.

The King Family Tree

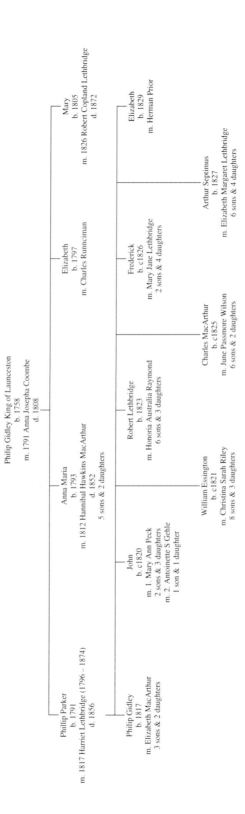

Philip Gidley King of Launceston
b. 1758
m. 1791 Anna Josepha Coombe
d. 1808

Phillip Parker
b. 1791
m. 1817 Harriet Lethbridge (1796 – 1874)
d. 1856

Anna Maria
b. 1793
m. 1812 Hannibal Hawkins MacArthur
d. 1852
5 sons & 2 daughters

Elizabeth
b. 1797
m. Charles Runnciman

Mary
b. 1805
m. 1826 Robert Copland Lethbridge
d. 1872

Philip Gidley
b. 1817
m. Elizabeth MacArthur
3 sons & 2 daughters

John
b. c1820
m. 1. Mary Ann Peck
2 sons & 3 daughters
m. 2. Antoinette S Gehle
1 son & 1 daughter

William Essington
b. c1821
m. Christina Sarah Riley
8 sons & 3 daughters

Robert Lethbridge
b. 1823
m. Honoria Australia Raymond
6 sons & 3 daughters

Charles MacArthur
b. c1825
m. June Passmore Wilson
6 sons & 2 daughters

Frederick
b. c1826
m. Mary Jane Lethbridge
2 sons & 4 daughters

Arthur Septimus
b. 1827
m. Elizabeth Margaret Lethbridge
6 sons & 4 daughters

Elizabeth
b. 1829
m. Herman Prior

The Australian Lethbridges (Tregeare Branch)

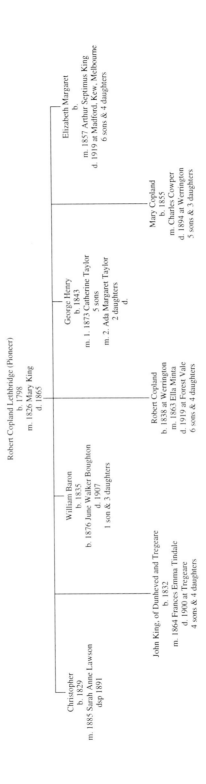

Robert Copland Lethbridge (Pioneer)
b. 1798
m. 1826 Mary King
d. 1865

Christopher
b. 1829
m. 1885 Sarah Anne Lawson
dsp 1891

William Baron
b. 1835
b. 1876 June Walker Boughton
d. 1907
1 son & 3 daughters

John King, of Dunheved and Tregeare
b. 1832
m. 1864 Frances Emma Tindale
d. 1900 at Tregeare
4 sons & 4 daughters

George Henry
b. 1843
m. 1. 1873 Catherine Taylor
5 sons
m. 2. Ada Margaret Taylor
2 daughters
d.

Robert Copland
b. 1838 at Werrington
m. 1863 Ella Minta
d. 1919 at Forest Vale
6 sons & 4 daughters

Mary Copland
b. 1855
m. Charles Cowper
d. 1894 at Werrington
5 sons & 3 daughters

Elizabeth Margaret
b.
m. 1857 Arthur Septimus King
d. 1919 at Madford, Kew, Melbourne
6 sons & 4 daughters

IN SUNDRY PLACES

Chapter 15 - A New Life

John King Lethbridge followed in his father's footsteps, not only in his choice of career but also in his public life. He was a well known figure in Launceston and was for many years Chairman of the Quarterly Sessions in East Cornwall. When William Baron died in March 1827 John King and Elizabeth Ann, who inherited the Tregeare estate by his death, moved almost immediately into Tregeare House, and it would seem that up to that point they had been living at Madford, and that his father Christopher had moved out, for we are told that the latter moved back into Madford at the same time. But where Christopher had been living is not at present known, unless it was at Tregeare.

His marriage to Elizabeth Ann Baron lasted for fourteen years but it was dogged by her ill-health, and the loss of both her sons at an early age must have been a great sadness to them. Two years after her death in 1833 he married again, his bride being Emma Palmer, daughter of the Rev. E. Palmer of Worcestershire. They met at Werrington while she was on a visit to her sister who had married Rev. H. A. Simcoe of Penheale. Werrington Park was the seat of the Duke of Northumberland, and for some years John King Lethbridge had been Steward of the Duke's Cornish and Devon properties, possible succeeding his father Christopher. In one of her letters to her husband his sister Harriet had written:

> "You will have heard that John has succeeded to the Stewardship, and he is also employed at the Admiralty about the Signals, by which he will get something."

His second marriage was more fruitful than the first and produced six children as shown in Lethbridge Family tree No.2.

Emma Palmer was a strong and forceful character with somewhat advanced religious convictions which other members of the family considered controversial. Millicent Lethbridge, who was her

Lethbridge Family Tree No. 2

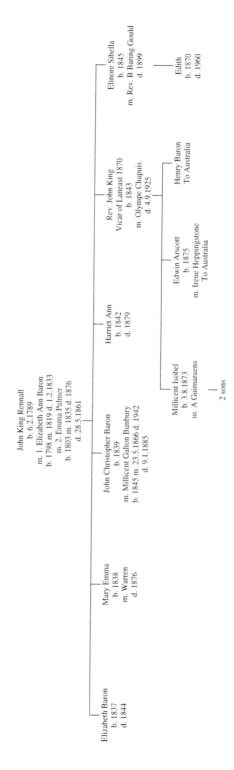

John King Rennall
b. 6.2.1789
m. 1. Elizabeth Ann Baron
b. 1798 m. 1819 d. 12.1833
m. 2. Emma Palmer
b. 1803 m. 1835 d. 1876
d. 28.5.1861

Elizabeth Baron
b. 1837
d. 1844

Mary Emma
b. 1838
m. Warren
d. 1876

John Christopher Baron
b. 1839
m. Millicent Galton Bunbury
b. 1845 m. 23.5.1866 d. 1942
d. 9.1.1885

Harriet Ann
b. 1842
d. 1879

Rev. John King
Vicar of Laneast 1870
b. 1843
m. Olympe Chapuis
d. 4.9.1925

Elinore Sibella
b. 1845
m. Rev. B Baring Gould
d. 1899

Millicent Isobel
b. 3.8.1873
m. A Guimaraens

Edwin Arscott
b. 1875
m. Irene Heppingstone
To Australia

Henry Baron
To Australia

Edith
b. 1870
d. 1960

2 sons

daughter-in-law, wrote a rather frank view of Emma's religious beliefs in her family history, but later deleted this section at the request of another member of the family who felt it might give offence.

When John King and Emma's first child was born they paid a delicate compliment to Elizabeth Ann Baron his first wife by naming the girl Elizabeth and adding Baron as an additional Christian name. She was the only female to be thus honoured though it ultimately became a tradition in the family for the males to be given this additional Christian name. This has persisted for several generations and in some cases Baron has become the first name, so that though the surname of Baron died out at Tregeare with the death of William Baron in 1827 the name has been by no means forgotten.

After becoming the owner of Tregeare John King Lethbridge embarked on a policy of increasing his estate through acquisitions, and during the next few years he purchased several additional parcels of land. He established a new and vigorous life at Tregeare, for he was young and energetic, could see the potential in his new environment, and was determined to exploit it to the full.

By the years 1839-40, when the Tithe Acts were in full swing and reliable surveys were carried out into land ownership, his holdings in the two principal Cornish parishes in which he was interested, were as follows –

The Tregeare Estate in 1839-40
In Egloskerry Parish

	A	.R	.P.
Part Tredundle	30	2	5
West Downend	220	0	33
Under Down	1	3	2
Tregeare	133	0	16
Hooper's or Adam's Tregeare	31	1	19
Little Penheale and Dawland	7	0	39
Hornabrook's Tregeare	35	0	31
Part Tregeare, Commons, Waste, & Roads	5	2	38
Tregeare Down	294	0	18
	756	8	21

In Laneast Parish

Tresparne	34	1	24
Down Park	2	2	24
Higher East Ground	3	2	3
Tresparne Down	13	3	4
Parmory	5	2	11
Tor Park	10	1	7
Bad Gall	117	1	36
Tregeare	112	3	21
Lidcott	185	3	27
High Hall	240	0	25
Duke's Hill	2	1	23
Commons	403	3	20
	1132	3	25

Total Acreage: 1891 – 0 – 6
(hectares: 765 – 28)

In his religious beliefs John King took after his mother and he has been described as an evangelical Christian. He supported the parish church of St. Mary Magdalene in Launceston and erected a four-light window in the South Aisle in memory of his father and mother and two uncles. The inscriptions read as follows –

Christopher Lethbridge, Gent, died 15 October 1830 aged 69.
Mary his wife whose maiden name was Copland died
30 December 1825 aged 66.

Lieutenant General Robert Lethbridge died 5 January 1831
aged 71.

The Rev. Charles Lethbridge died 14 December 1840 aged 77.

This window is erected to their memory by John King Lethbridge,
the eldest son of the above named Christopher Lethbridge.

When John King died on May 28 1861 aged seventy two he was buried in Egloskerry Churchyard in a large new square tomb surrounded by a granite kerb and quite close to the single yew tree to the north of the church. He is the first to be interred in this grave and occupies the centre section. His inscription is simple and just announces his name and date of death, but it is followed by a scriptural text that begins "Blessed are the dead who die in the Lord."

The remains of John King Lethbridge's fine tomb
in Egloskerry Churchyard

Towards the end of his life John King Rennall was obliged by poor health and failing eyesight to retire from public life, but on his death in 1861 the Royal Cornwall Gazette had much to say about him.

"This gentleman, so long known and so respected, as the Chairman of the County Quarter Sessions, died on the 27th May, after a very short illness, at Weston-Super-Mare, where he had gone for the benefit of his health…He is best known in the County as the Chairman of Quarter Sessions, in which his legal knowledge, his sound judgement, and his high principles, made him a most valuable officer, and obtained for him the confidence of all. On his retirement from that post through failing sight at the Michaelmas Sessions of 1858, the

Magistrates unanimously voted him an address expressing deep regret for his resignation and its course, gratitude for his services, and admiration of his character."

The report goes on to record another debt owed to him –

"Besides these services to his neighbours and his County, he conferred an obligation on the Nation and on Science, by the judicious and kind protection which he afforded to the illustrious Astronomer John Couch Adams, at that critical period of his early life, when the career of a greatly talented boy may be determined by the direction and encouragement he receives. The father of Adams was a moorland tenant of Mr. Lethbridge with a very large family; and when the extraordinary abilities of the son attracted attention in his remote and limited sphere, the judgement, encouragement and patronage of the landlord were most usefully exerted on his behalf."

So ended the life of a man who brought stability back to Tregeare. When he first came upon the scene all was uncertainty and worry, the last of the Barons were struggling with failing health, and the aftermath of their financial problems. The happiness of his first marriage was gradually dissipated and at one time grief must have seemed to be unending. But John King rose above all his troubles, preserved his faith in God, and settle down to make something of his life. His second marriage was a great success, and by the end of his life balance, calm and stability had been restored.

The Lethbridge Shield in the church

Although John King Rennall Lethbridge was buried in a fine new tomb in Egloskerry Churchyard his passing also signalled the end of an era, for changes were inevitably taking place. He was not only the first Lethbridge to own Tregeare, but he was also the last direct link with the Barons, and for centuries the Baron family had been firmly rooted in Egloskerry parish. But now the emphasis was changing, and forces were pulling in an opposite direction, towards the parish of Laneast. Even the new Tregeare House itself, although only a few hundred yards from Old Tregeare, had been built just over the parish boundary and was no longer in Egloskerry.

IN SUNDRY PLACES

Chapter 16 - Laneast

Laneast is a secluded and charming little hamlet situated about two miles to the south of Tregeare, and only about half a mile from the A395 highway which is its principal link with civilisation, and along which the occasional traffic whistles at an alarming rate. This half a mile however is enough to insulate it from some of the terrors of our present civilisation, and its character probably has not changed all that much in the last two hundred years or so. In fact Laneast displays many of the characteristics of the best type of Cornish village, namely peace, quiet, a calm satisfaction with the natural beauty of its surroundings, and the overall and abiding wisdom of the years.

It would be a mistake to think that this means there is no life in Laneast, for this would be very far from the truth. Life is indeed abundant and throbbing, and much of it centres, as it has done for the last several hundred years, in the church. The name of Laneast of course gives itself away, for 'Lan' in Cornwall means 'a holy place'.

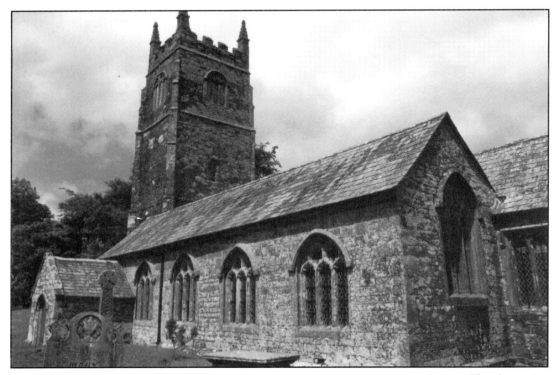

Laneast Church, exterior

The second element of the name usually represents the name of the Saint to whom the Church is dedicated but here there is a problem since the Saint's name was originally Sativola. This was later converted to Sidwell, which has remained to this day, but it is a little difficult to follow the conversion any further. Let it suffice that this beautiful little church, now mainly 15th century in character, but so old as to be awe-inspiring is a very special place and proof beyond doubt of the divine existence.

Laneast Parish covers around two thousand, five hundred acres and its population is something under two hundred. A glance at the Ordnance Survey Map is illuminating and rewarding as it shows that to the south Laneast is ringed by farms, settlements, hamlets, call them what you will, all starting with the Cornish prefix 'tre'. These include Trefranck, Trevenn, Tremeer, Trewithen, Trecollas, Tregunnon, Treroose, Trespearne, Trekenner, Trenarrett, Trethinna and Trewen. To the north is the high ground of Laneast Down, and almost exactly two miles away in that direction is the largest house in the area, Tregeare. To the east, and only a mile and a half away is the village of St. Clether with its sprinkling of Holy Wells and Celtic Crosses. Laneast does of course have its own Holy Well and Celtic cross, and is indeed a quite remarkable little hamlet.

Its connection with Tregeare goes back a long way and received a significant boost in the 17th century when the Edgcombes, who leased the manor, bought Old Tregeare Mansion House. Three generations of Edgcombes lived at Tregeare between 1635 and 1740 and only fifty years after their departure Jasper Baron was building his new house nearby and actually just inside the Laneast parish boundary. Round about 1770 the manor of Laneast was bought by William Rowe, and later his son Roger held it jointly with William Baron. The Rowes had long been closely related to the Barons, for Sarah Baron, daughter of John Baron of Treludick, and sister of George Baron, the merchant, had in 1650 married a William Rowe. Sarah was a favourite sister of George's and her husband was appointed joint executor of George's Will. In 1664 William Rowe together with Richard Short and Degory Baron compiled the Inventory of John Baron of Treludick, and William was also a witness to the marriage settlement between Joan Baron and William Saltern in 1684. It may well be that it was George Baron's money that funded the purchase of a share in the manor of Laneast.

Two of the most important farms lying between Laneast and Tregeare are Lidcott and High Hall, and both were absorbed into the growing

Tregeare Estate. Lidcott achieved national fame as the birthplace of John Couch Adams and had been in the possession of his family for a considerable time, and high Hall had belonged for several centuries to the Squire family.

There is a record of a Degory Squire owning High Hall at the beginning of the 17th century, and of continuous ownership until 1733 when, in the Will of Arthur Squire he left all his property to the Rev. John Baron of Wanstead in Essex, to sell at the best rate obtainable. As previously noted the Rev. John had already given up his interest in the Cornish estates in favour of his younger brother Degory, but it would seem likely that the Baron's retained an interest in part of High Hall for there is a Deed of Sale dated 5th August 1835 in which John King Lethbridge and John L. Cowlard purchased several properties and parcels of land including "a moiety of High Hall in Laneast." In the Tithe Redemption Survey of 1839/40 High Hall is shown as belonging to John King Lethbridge.

Two other national figures who brought fame to Laneast were John and Charles Wesley, both of whom preached in St. Sidwell's Church. John Wesley in particular enjoyed his several visits to Laneast and refers to them in his Journal, one such entry reading –

> "Monday April 16, 1744. In the afternoon we came again to Trewint. I learned that notice had been given of my preaching that evening in Laneast Church, which was crowded exceedingly. Mr. Bennett, the Minister of Laneast, carried me afterwards to his house, and (though above seventy years old) came with me in the morning to Trewint, where I had promised to preach at five."

In an excellent booklet giving the history of St. Sidwell's of Laneast the author, the Rev. T. S. Groser, who was Vicar from 1939 to 1950 makes the following interesting and significant statement concerning John Wesley –

> "It is well for us to remember, in fairness to him, that almost on his deathbed he made this solemn declaration – frequently made previously, in similar terms, in his sermons and conferences – "I never had any design of separating from the Church. I have no such design now. I declare once more that I live and die a member of the Church of England, and that none who regard my judgement or advice, will ever separate from it."

It seems little short of a calamity for the cause of Christian unity that, despite his frequent warnings, and declarations of loyalty to the English Church, John Wesley's great work should have been marred – after his death – by separatism and disunity, if not by (formal) schism."

Jasper Baron served as Churchwarden at Laneast in 1798, the very year he died, and he was in fact not only the first Baron to play an active part in the life of St. Sidwell's Church but also the last. In 1800 the five bells in the tower had to be rehung, but the timberwork of the bell chamber was found to be rotten and the bells were silent for the next twenty years.

On January 12, 1819 John King Rennall Lethbridge married Elizabeth Ann Baron at St. Sidwell's and the rejoicing that took place on that occasion may well be imagined. Unfortunately this was not to be the beginning of a series of happy Lethbridge events for when Elizabeth Ann died in 1833 she was buried in the Baron family vault under the chancel in Egloskerry Church, and it was not until January 31, 1837 that the Registers could record the baptism of Elizabeth Baron Lethbridge the firstborn of John King Rennall and his second wife Emma Palmer. Alas this was also to have a tragic sequel for in 1844 Elizabeth died in her eighth year and is commemorated in a plaque in Egloskerry Church.

In the same year, 1844, Mr Lethbridge who was the Patron of the Living, donated a piece land for a new Vicarage, and also subscribed £300 towards the cost of building which was estimated to be £580. The priest-in-charge at the time was the Rev. William Cowlard who was married to Mr Lethbridge's sister Sarah. A point of further interest is that the builder of the Vicarage was William Burt who is also reputed to have built Tregeare House.

Prior to 1866 St. Sidwell's was always in the care of a 'Perpetual Curate' but at this date the first Vicar, Rev. George Buckmaster Gibbons was installed. Three years later he obligingly stood down to allow John King Rennall Lethbridge's younger son, also called John King Lethbridge, to take his place, and this Rev. Mr Lethbridge was Vicar for the next six years before taking up a post as Chaplain to the Forces.

In 1885 Edward Galton Baron Lethbridge of Tregeare became Churchwarden at the age of eighteen and served continuously in this office until his death in 1932. Also in 1885 a brass tablet was erected

Left:
The Church,
St. Sidwell's
Church, Laneast

Right:
The Lethbridge
Thanksgiving
Window

Left:
An ancient
carved pew end

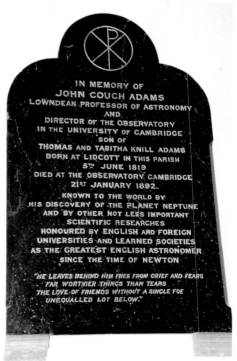

Right:
Memorial tablet
to John Couch
Adams

Edward Galton Baron Lethbridge and his Harriers

on the north wall of the chancel bearing the following inscriptions –

> "...in loving memory of his Father and Mother, John King and Emma Lethbridge; his sisters, Mary Emma Warren and Harriet Ann Lethbridge; and his only brother, John Christopher Baron Lethbridge. This tablet is erected in the year of our Lord 1885, by J. K. Lethbridge, M..A., Chaplain to Her Majesty's Forces, and formerly Vicar of this Parish A. D. 1870-76..."

When he was in residence at Tregeare Edward Lethbridge was a regular worshipper at St. Sidwell's and a great supporter of the Church. At the age of twenty-three he presented a brass cross and candlesticks for the altar and also replaced some of the slate flooring with tiling. Another Lethbridge memorial is the south-east three light window which commemorates three members of the family who survived the South African War. These were Captain John Guy Baron Lethbridge, Royal Artillery 3rd Hussars, who lost his right arm in the struggle, Captain Robert Christopher Baron Lethbridge, 5th Fusiliers, Charles Francis Baron Lethbridge, South African Constabulary, and also Major Alexander James King D. S. O., the King's Own Regiment. This window was dedicated on November 2, 1902.

In 1924 a sixth bell was added to the Tower, this being the gift of Mr & Mrs Edward Lethbridge, and bell ringing continued to be an essential part of village life, as it still is today. But a survey of the tower in 1938 reported problems with the bell frame and supporting beams necessitating a considerable amount of renovation. This problem was solved as were others as time marched on and Lethbridge succeeded Lethbridge at Tregeare. The day came, as inevitably it had to, when the Lethbridge ownership of Tregeare came to an end, and this was indeed a sad day for St. Sidwells and Laneast, for they had proved to be a principal mainstay of the village.

But as so frequently happens in life the ending of one chapter, calamitous though it may seem at the time, is often the signal for a new one to open. And so it has been with Laneast and its ancient Church. St. Sidwell's has served this small community faithfully and well for a thousand years, and has always found someone willing and able to carry on the tradition. And now as we enter a new Millennium it will continue to do so. The bells will still ring out.

IN SUNDRY PLACES

Chapter 17 - Full Bloom

With the succession of John Christopher Baron Lethbridge to the Tregeare and London Estates in 1861 the Lethbridge plant could be said to be in full flower. To continue the analogy a little further his father had proved to be an excellent plantsman. When John King had inherited Tregeare he had found that much needed doing, the plant was alive, but ailing, and desperately in need of a little tender loving care. And this is exactly what John King Rennall had given it. After the death of his first wife he had retired from his lawyer's practice and had devoted the whole of his time to the management of his estates. He had watered the plant and fed it and above all cared for it and encouraged it to grow.

And it had blossomed, so that when John Christopher succeeded him the Estate was something to be proud of. He also inherited from his father a splendid public reputation. His father had played a leading part in the life of the district, and John Christopher at the age of twenty two found this to be of great value. It was not long before he was appointed a Justice of the Peace, and he became Chairman of the Board of Guardians and Highway Board, and also one of the trustees of the Launceston Savings Bank.

In 1862 John Christopher Baron Lethbridge – who incidentally was known by his third Christian name of 'Baron' – was paid a visit at Tregeare by a Mrs Millicent Adele Galton Bunbury of Swansea, and this apparently simple social visit was to have a profound effect on his life. Mrs Bunbury was a widow and had two young and beautiful daughters, and like all mothers similarly endowed was hoping that one day they would each find a suitable husband, preferably refined, well connected and rich. Whether she was expecting this to happen at Tregeare is of course not known, but there is no doubt that young Mr Baron Lethbridge matched the specification exactly.

Her daughter Millicent was seventeen years old at the time, beautiful and nubile, and Baron experienced an attack of love at first sight. He invited Millicent to let him show her his rose garden, and here in this romantic spot he wasted no time but proposed to her. Millicent was suitably demure but practical and hurried back into the house to tell her mother, and to ask for instructions as to how to proceed. Mrs Bunbury's exact words of advice were known only to Millicent, but

*Ada Dorothy Ida King, wife of E.G.B. Lethbridge
and their three children, John, Dorothy and James*

Greystones

*Greystones gateposts,
all that is left of Old Tregeare*

The rose garden today

Lethbridge Family Tree No. 3

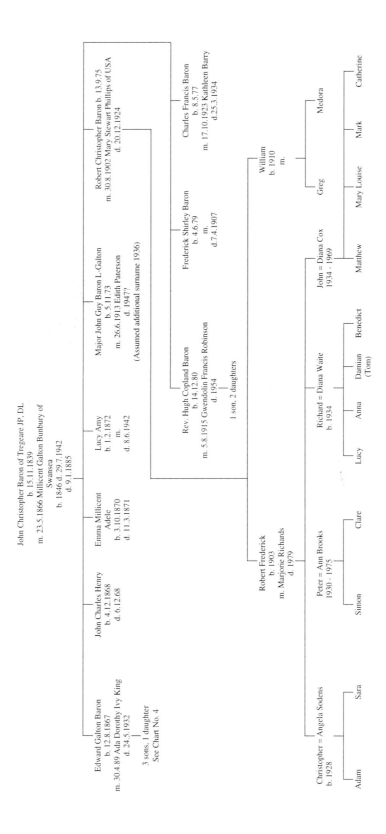

John Christopher Baron of Tregeare JP, DL
b. 15.11.1839
m. 23.5.1866 Millicent Galton Bunbury of
Swansea
b. 1846 d. 29.7.1942
d. 9.1.1885

Edward Galton Baron
b. 12.8.1867
m. 30.4.89 Ada Dorothy Ivy King
d. 24.5.1932

3 sons, 1 daughter
See Chart No. 4

John Charles Henry
b. 4.12.1868
d. 6.12.68

Emma Millicent
Adele
b. 3.10.1870
d. 11.3.1871

Lucy Amy
b. 1.2.1872
m.
d. 8.6.1942

Major John Guy Baron L-Galton
b. 5.11.73
m. 26.6.1913 Edith Paterson
d. 1947?
(Assumed additional surname 1936)

Robert Christopher Baron b. 13.9.75
m. 30.8.1902 Mary Stewart Phillips of USA
d. 20.12.1924

Charles Francis Baron
b. 8.5.77
m. 17.10.1923 Kathleen Barry
d.25.3.1934

Rev. Hugh Copland Baron
b. 14.12.80
m. 5.8.1915 Gwendolin Francis Robinson
d. 1954

1 son, 2 daughters

Frederick Shirley Baron
b. 4.6.79
m.
d.7.4.1907

William
b. 1910
m.

Robert Frederick
b. 1903
m. Marjorie Richards
d. 1979

Greg   Medora

Mary Louise   Mark   Catherine

Peter = Ann Brooks
1930 - 1975

John = Diana Cox
1934 - 1969

Simon   Clare

Matthew

Christopher = Angela Sodens
b. 1928

Richard = Diana Waite
b. 1934

Lucy   Anna   Damian   Benedict
              (Tom)

Adam   Sara

the message came over loud and clear. It was "grab him!" Four years later they were married.

On the face of it it was an ideal match, and the marriage was certainly fruitful for they produced nine children, only two of whom failed to survive childhood. Of the other seven, six were boys, and there is more to say about some of them later, but first let us look a little closer at Millicent who was a remarkable woman. It is rather strange how the story of Tregeare is sprinkled with extraordinary women, and this is a feature that has continued right up to the present day. For example, there was Joan Sleeman who married John Baron of Treludick at the beginning of the 17th century and was the mother of George Baron; there was Harriet Lethbridge who helped to found the Lethbridges of Australia; and in 1866 there was now Millicent Galton Bunbury who lived to be nearly a hundred years old.

She was twenty one when she married, and her husband was twenty seven, but in many ways they were an ill-assorted couple. He was a country gentleman, a typical huntin', shootin', and fishin' type, whose interests probably did not extend much further than Launceston his local town. But Millicent was entirely different, she had a keen and enquiring mind, which she had probably inherited from her mother, she could speak French and German fluently, and she enjoyed above all things the company and conversation of scientists and intellectuals. She was in fact a cousin of Charles Darwin which may explain why she had this leaning towards science. Her mother's family, the Galtons, were Quakers who are believed to have made their money by arms trading until this fact was discovered by the Society of Friends, to whom this trade was anathema.

But Millicent must have loved living at Tregeare – who could not? – though to one with such an active mind and a need for intellectual conversation boredom must at times have been hard to keep at bay. She occupied her mind by starting to write about the Lethbridge family and continued for many years. Ultimately she produced a large book which she also profusely illustrated in a very competent manner. In January 1904 her eldest son Edward Galton Baron had the book professionally bound and describes it in his diary as "a really wonderful production." The book is still extant and it has been possible to make one or two extracts from it thanks to Mr David and Mr Andrew Lethbridge.

Besides writing her family history Millicent also kept a Journal which too has survived though no longer in Cornwall, and she obviously found writing to be an outlet for her artistic talents. She made friends with local families, one of the principal ones being the Simcoe's of Penheale who were related to her husband by marriage, and she has left a short account of her friendship with them in the years following her marriage in 1866. Mrs Diana Colville, of Penheale, has kindly made this available, and in it Millicent describes the changes that inevitably took place after the Rev. Mr Simcoe's death. The Manor of Penheale is of course the most important land-holding in the area, having been here since before the Norman Conquest.

Meanwhile Baron and Millicent were settling down at Tregeare, and to mark the year of their marriage Baron rebuilt The Lodge in Tregeare village at the entrance to his drive to the house. This was known as North Lodge to distinguish it from South Lodge in Piper's Pool at the end of the long South Drive. A stone bearing his initials and the date was inserted into the gable end of the Lodge.

North Lodge, built by Baron Lethbridge in 1866

In 1870, as reported in a previous chapter, Baron's only brother John King was installed as Vicar of Laneast, and this strengthened the link between St Sidwell's and Tregeare. All Baron and Millicent's children were baptised here, but there is no mention in the church records of any other involvement by the parents. However, in other directions

Baron's career was developing, and in 1874 he had the honour of being appointed High Sheriff of Cornwall. He was also appointed a Deputy Lieutenant of the County.

A few years later in 1879 Baron Lethbridge built the house Greystones overlooking Tregeare Green, and we are indebted to the present owner Dr Jim Burridge for the splendid aerial photograph and for permission to explore his garden. It would appear that Old Tregeare House was immediately behind Greystones and in fact was not finally demolished until the year 1900. Dr Burridge has recently constructed an ornamental pond behind the house and mentioned that he had difficulty with this as there was an accumulation of builder's rubble immediately under the surface. This would seem to corroborate the theory.

The photograph also provides other clues to the existence of the previous house. The rectangular shape of the site can be clearly seen, and also the walled garden on the right hand side of the picture. In the top right hand corner can be seen the shell of another small building which gives the impression of being once two stories high. This could have perhaps been a barn though there is a lancet window remaining which seems a little too grand for such a building. Could it have been a chapel, one wonders, and if so is it too fanciful to suggest this may have originally been the "Chapel of Tregeare" mentioned on page 19.

Old Tregeare's front door archway, now between the greenhouses at Tregeare House

A further interesting feature of Greystones is the massive stone pillars at the front entrance which Dr Burridge believes are older than the house. These are flanked on either side by about thirty six feet of low wall which at one time contained iron railings, some of which still remain and the supports have interesting ornate finials. The gate posts are wide enough apart to take a small carriage and it is interesting to note that they would have been in alignment with a drive coming up from South Lodge and through the avenue of oaks at the entrance to the village.

Another little snippet of news concerning Baron Lethbridge is contained in the Cornwall and Devon Post of 29 March 1879. This says –

> "At the annual meeting of Launceston Cricket Club, Mr J.C. Baron Lethbridge was elected President and Mr G.G. White captain."

A photograph of Baron at around this time shows him to have been good looking with a fine head of hair and a somewhat straggly moustache and beard.

In 1880 the Lethbridges suffered a family bereavement when a cousin of Baron's, who had also been christened John Christopher, died while staying at Tregeare. This cousin lived in London, at Granville House, Blackheath, and a brass tablet in the chancel of Egloskerry church states that he died on 27 August 1880 aged sixty four years. It is probably due to the similarity of their names that decided Baron's parents to use his third Christian name for their son.

John Christopher was married to Mary Pridham who also later was buried in Egloskerry churchyard. She died on 15 February 1899 aged eighty three. Her grave is situated alongside the larger vault of the Tregeare Lethbridges, and has a cross headstone bearing her name. Next to her are three grave plots without stones and then a fourth one which carries the inscription reading

> "Caroline Mary, daughter of John Christopher Lethbridge and Mary Pridham his wife. Died 24 March 1922 aged 80."

Egloskerry Church has a beautiful east window over the altar and this is dedicated to John Christopher Lethbridge and Mary his wife and was erected by their son Christopher in 1906. A small window in the north wall of the Chancel is dedicated to Christopher Lethbridge by his wife, and he died on 11 July 1910.

The Census records for 1881 detail composition of the household at Tregeare for everyone living in the house had to be listed, and this is an illuminating document as it indicates the lifestyle adopted by Baron and Millicent and the comparatively large number of personal servants they employed. The list is as follows.

Name	Position	Marriage	Age	Description	Birthplace
John C.B. Lethbridge	Head	Mar.	41	Magistrate	Laneast
Millicent Lethbridge	Wife	Mar.	35		Swansea, Wales
Susan M. Chrisp	Governess	Unm.	28		Ryde, I.O.W
Lucy A. Lethbridge	Dau.		9		Laneast
John G.B. Lethbridge	Son		7		Laneast
Robert C.B. Lethbridge	Son		5		Laneast
Charles F.B. Lethbridge	Son		3		Laneast
Frederic S.B. Lethbridge	Son		1		Laneast
Hugh C.B. Lethbridge	Son		3m		Laneast
Emelin Northey	Servant	Wid.	46	Nurse	Trewen
Margaret P. Westlake	Servant	Unm.	19	Housemaid	Trewen
Sophia Spry	Servant	Unm.	25	Housemaid	Jacobstow
Martha Parr	Servant	Unm.	45	Cook	St. Giles, Devon
Jane Turner	Servant	Unm.	17	Nursemaid	Liskeard
Fanny Bray	Servant	Unm.	18	Kitchen maid	Bolventor
Lavinia Poulmounter	Servant	Unm.	28	Laundry maid	St. Austell
John Ryle	Servant	Unm.	29	Butler	Padstow
William Jeffery	Servant	Unm.	30	Coachman and Groom	Egloskerry

This is an impressive list of "Living –in" servants all of whom received their keep as part of their wages. There is no information as to what their wages were, but in a similar household in the Isle of Wight at a slightly earlier time the Butler was being paid sixty guineas per annum, the Coachman forty guineas, Cook twenty guineas, Nurse twenty two guineas, Housemaid and Kitchen maid twelve guineas etc., etc. (and some of the latter had to "find their own tea"!)

With the benefit of hindsight one wonders whether in keeping such an opulent establishment Baron Lethbridge was not sowing the seeds of disaster, for though wages were not high he was spending freely in other directions. And of course the one event that he could not possible have forseen was his own death within the next few years, for this evoked a punishing attack of death duty. Indeed, it is now possible to say that death duties exacted during the next hundred years were a contributory and major cause of the Lethbridge's finally having to give up Tregeare.

The Fates were indeed unkind to the Lethbridges of Tregeare in the hundred years beginning 1885 and they suffered the loss of a large part of their material possessions. At the beginning of the period Baron and Millicent Lethbridge were living a life of considerable comfort in their beautiful home, surrounded by servants and at least with all the appearances of wealth, and at the end of it there was nothing. Land was sold off and the estate dwindled until only a few hundred acres were left. Rents were lost, income went down, and in the end even the house and its contents had to be sold at auction, a sad ending to one hundred and fifty years of Lethbridge management.

The process of decline began in January 1885 when Baron fell off his horse. He was out riding a favourite grey hunter when the horse stumbled and threw him. He quickly remounted, feeling none the worse for the accident, but only a few days later, sitting at home quietly one evening with Millicent he apparently dropped off to sleep, and it was a terrible shock to her to find that he had in fact died. He was only forty four years of age.

Sudden and painless death, though kind to the recipient, is always hard to bear by those who are left, and Millicent was not the only one to be shocked. The whole district was affected, and this may have contributed to the astonishing public display of concern shown at his funeral. No one in Tregeare had ever seen anything like this before, or since, nor is anyone likely to see anything like it again.

One newspaper account contains the following passage –

> "…The funeral was timed to leave Tregeare House (for Egloskerry parish church) at two o'clock, and for some time before that hour the grounds and approaches to the house, though situated in the midst of a rural district, were thronged with carriages and conveyances and groups of people on foot who had come from all parts of the countryside for the purpose of joining in the processions, notwithstanding the bleak and wintry aspect of the day…"

It goes on to report that there were sixty mourners on horseback, and they headed the procession, followed by a host of people on foot and in carriages and conveyances of various descriptions

> "Altogether the procession comprised, besides the hearse, fifty-two vehicles, forming an unbroken line of about a mile in length, whilst a number of persons on foot walked on either

146

side of the carriages, and groups of others wended their way independently to the church, two miles distant from the house."

Baron was buried in the Lethbridge family vault alongside his father, John King Rennall, and his two children who had died in their childhood. The horse, which was the unwitting cause of all this distress, was shot, which seem a rather harsh punishment for a simple stumble. But because it was an old friend of the family the hoofs were sent to London to be polished and the skin to the tanner to be made into a mat. The newspaper claims this as proof of Mr Lethbridge's kind and sympathetic feeling.

IN SUNDRY PLACES

Chapter 18 - The Head of the Family

Baron and Millicent Lethbridge had nine children in all, two of whom died in infancy and were buried in the Lethbridge vault in Egloskerry churchyard where they lie with their father and grandfather. Of the seven survivors six were boys, and Lucy Amy the only girl. As the only daughter it was perhaps inevitable that her mother should make a fuss of her, and she did in fact spend all her life as her mother's companion even to the extent of being educated at home, Millicent confessing that she could not spare her to go to school.

Lucy Amy Lethbridge,
Millicent's daughter and Companion

Robert Christopher Baron Lethbridge 1875 – 1924.
Courtesy of Richard Lethbridge.

At one time Amy found an interest in working for the Poor, especially in the East End of London, and her mother comments that "the many other amusements and pursuits into which she had entered with more than usual zeal lost their attraction" but she adds that Amy was not able to devote all her time to this work due to the many home duties of an only daughter and the sister of many brothers. One other interest was paramount in Amy's life, this being her religious beliefs, and in 1905 when she was in her thirties she was received into the Roman Catholic Church. Was this perhaps the ultimate rebellion?

Two years younger than Amy was John Guy Baron who was destined to become a soldier, and a very brave one too. He achieved the rank of Major, but in a bloody encounter with the Boers in the South African war he had the misfortune to lose his right arm. From the detailed account of his fight given by his mother in her book about the Lethbridges of Tregeare he was indeed lucky to have escaped with his life, a blessing later to be commemorated by the window in Laneast Church. In later life Guy added his grandmother's name of Galton to his own and became known as Lethbridge-Galton.

Millicent Lethbridge writes an engaging account of her next son Robert Christopher Baron who as a child appears to have been as fearless as his elder brother Guy. At five years of age he survived s slide down the banisters that resulted in a drop of about twelve feet and a nasty gash on his head, and before he had fully recovered from this he managed to vault over the high nursery fender and land on the hearth only inches from a blazing fire and a boiling kettle.

His adventurous life continued and he too became a soldier and saw ample foreign service, being present at the famous battle of Omdurman and other trouble spots where the British Army was involved. He survived a serious attack of enteric fever in Crete, several battles in the South African Campaign, and also service in Antigua. For a time he was quartered in the Isle of Wight, which must have seemed strangely peaceful after all this activity overseas, and here he met an American girl, Mary Stewart Phillips, and married her in the delightful little parish church of Godshill in the Island.

Robert was an extremely good looking and dashing young officer; and he and his American bride made a handsome couple indeed. His good looks were inherited by his children, as was his love of an active life. His son Robert Frederick studied at the Camborne School of Mines and followed a gold mining career, and his other son William ultimately settled in the United States to which Mary Lethbridge returned after her husband's death at the comparatively early age of forty nine. It is to Mr Richard Lethbridge, son of Robert Frederick that we are indebted for information about this branch of the family. (See Lethbridge Family Tree No. 3).

Wedding of Robert Christopher Baron Lethbridge to Mary Phillips of U.S.A., August 1902, Godshill, I.O.W. 7th from left John Guy B.L., 8th from left Lucy Amy Lethbridge, 9th the Bride, 10th the Groom, 12th Groom's Mother Millicent Galton Baron Lethbridge. Extreme right Edward Galton Baron Lethbridge of Tregeare, next to him his wife Ada Dorothy Ivy. Many of the guests were American.

When Millicent Lethbridge found herself a widow in 1885 at the age of forty she took a very courageous decision, which was perhaps misinterpreted by some. She came to the conclusion that to continue living at Tregeare in the style to which she had certainly become accustomed, and after payment of death duties, would seriously deplete the income necessary to give her six sons the sort of education she wished them to have, and she decided that their education was of paramount importance, and that it would be kinder to her children to reduce this standard of living while they were young.

So she decided to leave Tregeare and go to live in Switzerland where she had friends. She did not dispose of Tregeare but in fact left their eldest son Edward Galton Baron in charge but took with her the other five, and of course Amy. Edward was seventeen years old at the time and helped his mother to clear up at Tregeare and to set up her temporary home in Switzerland. He then went to a Tutor at Eggesford for two years to prepare him for entry into St John's College Oxford, his vacations being spent mainly with his mother but partly at Tregeare.

Edward Galton Baron Lethbridge as a young man

Edward went up to St. Johns in January 1887 but his stay there was comparatively short as he had a bad attack of measles in 1888 which affected his eyesight, leaving him unable to read, and it was some years before his eyes were better. He left Oxford and returned to Tregeare intending to stay there. His mother opposed this at first, partly because he was so young, and partly because she felt this period of enforced idleness should be used – as she put it – "to enable him to acquire elsewhere such general knowledge as would be of service to him afterwards as a country gentleman." But he showed such an aptitude for estate management and took his position so seriously that she had to admit later that he had done the right thing.

Edward had started to keep a diary when his mother left for Switzerland, and excerpts from this diary have been made available through the kindness and diligence of Mr Andrew Lethbridge. These entries show that he was an extremely self possessed young man, very conscious of his position in life, and very attached to Tregeare. His diary entries for Christmas 1886 tell their own story. He was nineteen years old and had decided to spend Christmas at Tregeare.

Monday December 20
> Thank God I am home again! Tregeare seems dearer than ever!

Wednesday December 22
> I visited every house in Badgall.
> All seem so pleased at the prospect of my spending Xmas among them.

Christmas Eve 1886
> Fine. After breakfast I was busy dispensing wine etc. to the poor and also I rode round and distributed all the "bread money". In the evening some Tregeare "singers" came round and sang five or six songs in the Servants Hall.

151

Saturday Christmas day 1886

> Fine and Bright. I walked to Laneast in the morning and took the sacrament. The church was very prettily decorated. I got home at 1-0 and after a few minutes went to the Servants Hall where Blatchford, Hake, Harry, Jeffery, C. Ball, and their respective families (19 souls in all) had assembled. After the usual "few words" I retired, and had my solitary Christmas dinner in the study.

In August 1888 Edward came of age and his proud mother reports at some length that the festivities at Tregeare went on for three days. They were almost of a feudal nature with presentations from tenants, Launceston tradesmen and the parishes of Egloskerry and Laneast.

> "speeches were touching in their kindness and loyalty, testifying to the affection and respect which had been bestowed during so many years on the grandfather and father being now carried to the son."

The kennels, restored in 1998

It was in this year that Edward started his pack of harriers for which he became well known and which he kept for the next thirty years, giving him great pleasure. The harrier is a hound, slightly smaller and not quite so fast as the foxhound, used in hunting the hare, and providing splendid exercise for the followers.

Earlier in 1888 his mother came back from Switzerland having decided once more to live in England. Strangely enough she did not come back to Tregeare but decided to live in Clifton so that her sons could be educated at Clifton College. In 1891 Edward married, his bride being Ada Dorothy Ivy King, daughter of the Vicar of Werrington whom he had known since he was a boy. Millicent wrote rather a curious passage in her family history about this event.

The large stable block behind Tregeare House

"I wish I might here give a little biographical notice of my dear Ivy, as to her husband and children, for whom this book is written, she is by far the most important person therein. But what is a poor biographer to do if she is not allowed to say what she wishes? It must suffice that my dear daughter-in-law's life is written on the hearts of those who love her instead of on these pages…"

What Millicent meant by this cryptic remark can only be surmised though it is almost certainly a reference to something she wrote about

Emma Palmer, her mother-in-law and wife of John King Rennall Lethbridge who had controversial religious views. Whatever it was that Millicent wrote about her mother-in-law it upset her brother-in-law Rev. John King Lethbridge and at his request she obligingly expunged it from the record. It can hardly be imagined that she had anything controversial to say about her son's wife, but it would have been nice if she had shared it with us!

The weather on the day of Edward and Ivy's wedding was vile, but it cleared up at the right moment and Millicent was able to write

> "...the sun shone brilliantly on the bride as a true omen of the light she would bring into her new home."

Soon after the wedding Edward was appointed a Justice of the Peace for Cornwall, and it began to look as though the sun was to continue to shine, but alas on 12 March 1890 their first child was born and lived only for two days. A year later, almost to the day, a second son, John Edward, was born under very difficult and trying conditions which certainly did not augur well for the future.

Edward had to go to Exeter about a week before the baby was due, and while he was there it started to snow, the worst blizzard in living memory. He set off for home but only got as far as Okehampton before the roads became impassable, and there he was marooned for two days, very worried about Ivy's condition as she had not been well. After two days and in desperation he set off to walk and managed to drag himself ten miles, and finally reached home to find Ivy terribly alarmed and upset, not knowing what had happened to him. Two days later 'Jack' was born.

Round about this time Millicent's family book contains a rather wistful page showing a picture of Elinore Sibella Lethbridge, the youngest daughter of John King Rennall. She married Rev. B. Baring Gould and died following a holiday in the Tyrol and Switzerland where she contracted scarlet fever. Millicent says of her

> "As a girl her almost childish love of fun and apparent superficiality gave but little indication of what that character would develop into in afterlife – absolutely selfless, deeply religious without a trace of cant, pursuing the even tenor of her way.... All my sisters-in-law were dear to me, but not so dear as Elinore or so deeply mourned."

She follows this with a picture of Egloskerry Church and the following–

"I here finish the history of the Tregeare Lethbridges of my generation, but before I begin a new page and a new generation I feel inclined to insert a little picture of Egloskerry Church, which was perhaps more bound up with the affections of those who have now passed away, even than Laneast.

Tregeare lies partly in Egloskerry and partly in Laneast Parish and during Mr Simcoe's lifetime the Tregeare party used to go regularly to Egloskerry Church every Sunday morning and to Laneast every afternoon.

The family vault is at Egloskerry, and there rest my dear husband and two children, and my father and mother-in-law. Now that Mr Simcoe has long been dead and another generation sprung up to which the Egloskerry traditions no longer appeal with the same force, Laneast has become the Church to which my children bring their allegiance, and it is in the churchyard of Laneast that stands the little cross that marks my eldest grandchild's grave."

Edward Lethbridge's
Coming of Age Menu

IN SUNDRY PLACES

Chapter 19 - The Beginning of the End

The feudal nature of the Tregeare organisation continued and "Squire" Lethbridge remained popular, not only with his tenantry but also in Launceston where the scale of his public activities exceeded even his father's or grandfather's. His proud mother listed over sixteen organisations of which he was a member, and in many cases Vice Chairman or Chairman, and when the so-called Great War came along in 1914 she was able to add a further half dozen. With all this activity it is surprising that he had any home life at all, and there is no doubt that the stress of all the responsibilities he took on ultimately began to tell on his health and his ability to lead a normal life. It must be said too that Ivy also led a very energetic public life.

But at the time of Edward's marriage to Ivy little occurred to disturb the peaceful course of their lives, and two photographs have survived which are interesting in the context of the Tregeare story, the first of these being connected with Old Tregeare, the old Elizabethan mansion house that was vacated by the Barons when they built the present Tregeare House. This photograph has been mentioned before and a possible date of 1870-1875 has been given, though it may well have been taken later than this. See page 76.

The principal interest in this old photograph is the group of people standing outside the gates leading to the building – gate posts which are still there.

This group, comprising five men, three women and six children, is very similar to a group featured in the second photograph which was taken round about the same time and which turned up many years later in a local paper under the title "The Worthies of Tregeare." The newspaper was sufficiently intrigued to try and establish the identity of the men in the picture, and succeeded in naming them all. Millicent also reproduces this picture in her book together with the names of most of them – all but two of which agree.

THE WORTHIES OF TREGEARE

Originally in the collection of the late Major James Lethbridge, of Tregeare, this delightful period picture, taken sometime before the turn of the century, shows a group of men connected with the Tregeare Estate. With the aid of some of our older readers, including one lady of 94, we have been able to identify all of them: Back row, standing, left to right: —. Jeffery (groom), D. Jeffery, N. Jeffery, —. Hodge, H. G. Venning; middle row, seated, left to right: S. Gimblett, Henry Jenkin, John Sandercock, —. Blatchford (bailiff), H. Hawke (gamekeeper), M. Court (Under-Whip), Tom Davey (mason); seated on ground: Uriah Venning, Jack Willmott (Whip), Maj Lethbridge, who until 75 still rode regularly to hounds, remembered vividly the pack of harriers which, at the time of this picture, his father, the late Mr. E. G. B. Lethbridge, kept at Tregeare, as indicated by the Whipper-in and his assistant in the photograph.

The Worthies of Tregeare

Back Row, standing, Left to Right

William Jeffery (Groom)	Entered Tregeare service 1864
Richard Jeffery	Entered Tregeare service 1857
Edward Jeffery	
- Hodge or Tom Davy	
Henry Geake Venning	Entered Tregeare service 1853

Middle Row, sitting, Left to Right

Shilston Gimblett	
Henry Jenkins	Entered Tregeare service 1849
John Sandercock	Entered Tregeare service 1871
Samuel Blatchford (Bailiff)	Entered Tregeare service 1847 (?)
Richard Hawke (Gamekeeper)	Entered Tregeare service 1852
M. Court (Under Whip)	
Tom Davey	

Seated on ground

Uriah Venning
Jack Wilmott (Whip)

Edward and Ivy's next child was a daughter, Dorothy Mary Baron who ultimately succeeded to the control of Tregeare and lived there until her death in April 1973. And two years later in February 1894 their third son James Christopher Baron was born, a birth in which his mother nearly died. He too later inherited Tregeare from his sister and for a further seven years lived there until his death in 1980.

Lethbridge Family Tree No. 4

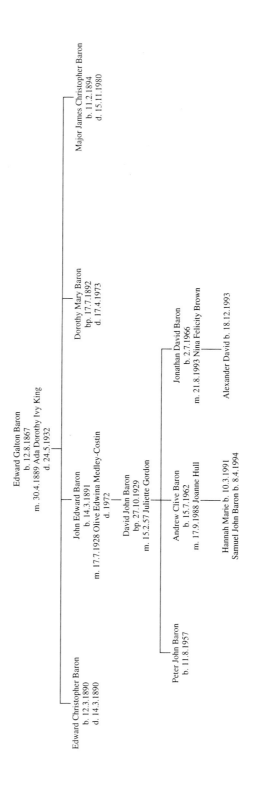

Edward Galton Baron
b. 12.8.1867
m. 30.4.1889 Ada Dorothy Ivy King
d. 24.5.1932

Edward Christopher Baron
b. 12.3.1890
d. 14.3.1890

John Edward Baron
b. 14.3.1891
m. 17.7.1928 Olive Edwina Medley-Costin
d. 1972

Dorothy Mary Baron
bp. 17.7.1892
d. 17.4.1973

Major James Christopher Baron
b. 11.2.1894
d. 15.11.1980

David John Baron
bp. 27.10.1929
m. 15.2.57 Juliette Gordon

Peter John Baron
b. 11.8.1957

Andrew Clive Baron
b. 15.7.1962
m. 17.9.1988 Joanne Hull

Jonathan David Baron
b. 2.7.1966
m. 21.8.1993 Nina Felicity Brown

Hannah Marie b. 10.3.1991
Samuel John Baron b. 8.4.1994

Alexander David b. 18.12.1993

But fundamental changes were on the way. When John Edward Baron grew up it became clear that he had not inherited his father's aptitude for estate management, and that it would not be possible for him to inherit the cares and responsibilities of the estate. This must have been a terrible blow to his father, whose health suffered accordingly, and he was faced with deciding what should be done to preserve the continuation of the Lethbridge inheritance. His solution was to form a Trust which would ensure that all his children were provided for and that Tregeare would remain under Lethbridge administration.

Millicent's family history at this point takes a curious philosophical turn. After reporting that within one month of "Jim's" birth his father Edward had a fall from his horse and dislocated his shoulder which caused him considerable pain and was a long time in healing, she writes –

> "Since then I do not think there have been any events worth recording here, the chief interest in these last years centring on the three little ones, who in their grandmother's eyes are very nearly perfection!"
> And here I cannot refrain from inserting my grandchildren's photo, although according to the plan of this book I ought to finish one generation before commencing another – But how can I resist the temptation, for the task of writing a record of those three lives will fall to other hands for that purpose – what will be written on those blank pages?..."

The photo she includes is dated 1903 and shows Dorothy aged eleven, John twelve and Jim aged nine, a typical posed group of three children of which any parent could be proud. Underneath this picture were two others, side by side. One had the caption

> "John E. B. Lethbridge on his pony "Toby" with his father, Edward G. B. Lethbridge, 1902"

and alongside it the other was captioned

> "Edward G. B. Lethbridge on his pony "Daisy" with his father J. C. Baron Lethbridge, 1873"

and Millicent had added the comment "History repeats itself."

History certainly seemed to be repeating itself, and there was no indication at this point that history was about to take an unexpected and savage turn that would ultimately lead to the end of the Lethbridge tenure of Tregeare. Millicent's book ceases to be a fount of inspiration and it maybe that as an extremely intelligent woman she appreciated that something was wrong and that the future would bring trouble to the family.

Whatever the reason she says little else about her son Edward, of whom she was so proud, or about her beloved daughter-in-law Ivy, except to record that in 1924 both Edward and Ivy had their portraits painted by Sir Arthur Cope R.A. and she lists in equal detail all the many organisations and committees to which they both belonged, but nothing at all about their lives and future problems which we, with the benefit of hind sight, now know existed. Nor does she record

anything further about her grandchildren John, Dorothy and Jim who remain central to the Tregeare story. Millicent did not die until 1942, at the great age of ninety seven, and Mr Richard Lethbridge who was born in 1934 remembers her as an old lady and says she was still of striking appearance and had obviously been very beautiful.

John, Dorothy & James bathing in the Pond

Edward kept his diary over the years, a habit he had acquired when his mother went to live in Switzerland soon after his father had died, and extracts from this have become an important source of information about life at Tregeare in the early years of the 20th century. He records the final days of Old Tregeare Mansion House and the erection of the front door archway in its present position between the greenhouses, and the ultimate demolition of the remains of the house is September 1900. In July 1902 the staircase window commemorating the building of the house by Jasper Baron in 1790 was fitted, and in October the same year the Thanksgiving Window was installed in Laneast Church.

There are several references in the diary to bathing in the pond with the children and also about stocking the pond with fish. The fact that the pond had to be restocked with fish from time to time suggests that perhaps the two activities did not really mix. There are frequent diary entries about the water supply to the house which was obviously a source of trouble. Particularly troublesome was the reservoir at Lidcot, so much so that Edward writes on October 16th 1901 – "Re the everlasting water supply question – I propose to do away with Lidcot reservoir." Apparently the other Tregeare reservoir was operating satisfactorily.

A couple of curious entries concern his "weeding out" of old deeds from the attic. Obviously he was not sure what to do about some of these, so he sought advice from his lawyer, Mr Grylls.

April 11th 1900   By 3.36 to Lanson and saw Grylls re destroying Deeds etc.,

April 12th 1900   Buried Deeds and papers in little Broomhill (right hand corner!)

Presumably Grylls advised him to take this odd course of action, and it would be very interesting to find these documents, but as in all stories of buried treasure there is a snag. The problem here is that in the Egloskerry Parish part of the Tregeare Estate there are six different fields called Broomhill, and in the Laneast part of the Estate there are no fewer than eight – and not one of these fourteen fields is called "Little" Broomhill. There are Outer, Higher, Middle, Lower and Long Broomhills, and several others, but no "Littles."

On a much more practical, but equally interesting, subject the diary records the opening on January 1st 1903 of "The Tregeare Reading Room and Institute, free to all Tenants and their families." This sounds like a very enlightened and progressive action on the part of a landlord, but there is no further information as to what was involved, nor as to where it was held.

Also in 1903 there is the following entry.

"August 24th. Piper came as Groom coachman at 17/- per week – house free."

The house was the Lodge – or North Lodge as it was in those days – and this was the start of a long collaboration between the Piper family and Tregeare. Mr and Mrs Piper had a daughter, Gladys, who was born at The Lodge in 1904, and when she left school automatically

Mr. & Mrs. Piper
at the front gate

went into service in Tregeare House. She worked for eleven and a half years as a laundry maid and ultimately married the gardeners boy. Now well into her nineties Gladys has revisited Tregeare a couple of times, and in spite of the inevitable changes that have taken place has recognised her old work place and has remembered much about life at Tregeare under Edward and Ivy Lethbridge.

Her father had two men working under him, and was responsible for eight hunters and two coach horses. The horses were dispersed in 1914, and in 1916 her father, who was in the army and in France, met a Captain who had been a schoolmaster at Camelford and who was riding Redwing, one of her father's previous charges. Mr Piper claimed afterwards that he rattled a bunch of keys and called the horse, and the horse recognised him.

Dorothy as a young girl
with her Mother Ivy

In its heyday before the first World War there were fifteen in Staff; in the kitchen a Cook, Kitchen maid, and tweeny maid, two other housemaids and a lady's maid, a Butler and two housemen, two laundry maids, and three gardeners. A dairymaid came in three times a week to make butter and cheese, and of course when the children were small they had a nursemaid or a governess. On the farm there were two men, two masons, two carpenters and two waggoners, and the Harriers found employment for a Whip and Under Whip and a gamekeeper. The Butler supervised in the house, and a Bailiff the outside staff.

The 1914-1918 War caused some shattering changes to be made to this "good old days" lifestyle and things were never quite the same again. The War in fact heralded the start of the social revolution that has continued to the present day, and may perhaps not event yet be over.

A few months before War was declared Edward and Ivy celebrated their Silver Wedding with a family party at Tregeare, and Millicent wrote the following little note about it.

> "April 30 1914 the 25th anniversary of my dear Edward's and Ivy's marriage. To celebrate this Silver Wedding I (together with Amy, Guy and Edie, and Hugh) are staying at Tregeare. At this happy Family gathering we have to regret dear Jim's absence with his tutor at Westgate, as well as that of Bob, Mary, and Frank, who are in America, and of Ivy's relations who are unfortunately not able to be with us on this joyful occasion."

N.B.

Amy = Lucy Amy Lethbridge (aged 42)

Guy = Major John Guy Baron Lethbridge)
) married 26/6/1913
Edie = Edith Paterson, his wife)

Hugh = Rev. Hugh Copland Baron Lethbridge (aged 34)

Jim = James Christopher Baron Lethbridge (aged 20)

Bob = Robert Christopher Baron Lethbridge)
) married 30/8/1902
Mary = Mary Stewart Phillips, his wife) in Godshill I.O.W

Frank = Charles Francis Baron Lethbridge (aged 37)

Is it significant that Millicent makes no mention of either Jack who was twenty three at the time, nor Dorothy who was 21? Jack's inability to play the role that had been expected of him, and to be trained to take over from his father in due course, was already apparent, and it did ultimately lead to a serious disagreement in the family, and contributed very greatly to his father's problems. But the omission of Dorothy's name from the above account is indeed strange, for when her father died in 1932 it was she who assumed control.

1918 was in some ways the climax of Edward's career, for it was in this year he was appointed High Sheriff of Cornwall, the greatest honour the county could bestow. But the year also marked the beginning of the end of the Lethbridge ownership of Tregeare although they continued in occupation for another fifty years. But at the end of the War Edward decided to sell off part of his estate, and within a year he had disposed of Trethorne, Gospenheale, Trespearne, Trekenna, Wollens, and Red Down. Over two thousand acres still remained but the sale indicated that all was not well.

Another major change in 1918 was to give up the Harriers which had been his pride and joy for so many years. He had contemplated this step as far back as 1907 due to the establishment of several other packs in the neighbourhood, but he had been persuaded to carry on by his supporters. Hunting had been his principal relaxation since 1885, though the War had curtailed the sport somewhat, but the economic situation now made it imperative to reduce expenditure and his declining health was an additional factor to be considered.

In the public sector his work load continued to be heavy though this too had to be gradually reduced. His record of service in the community was impressive to say the least, as for example by the time of his death he had been a county magistrate for forty years, with many years as Chairman of the Bench. He had been a member of the local Board of Guardians for forty three years, again serving for several years as Chairman. The problems associated with his health became more acute, but his death on 24th May 1932 at the age of 65 was a shock to everyone.

The local 'Post and Weekly News' published a long and eulogistic obituary in which the writer referred to the many public bodies of which he had been a member and had given loyal and continuous service, and expressed the view that he would be difficult to replace.

> "...if there was a man in this district who gave himself in good work for the public it was Mr Lethbridge. A Britisher to the backbone he was a fine representative of the land-owning class, and ever zealous for the welfare of those with whom he was brought into touch, whatever their positions in life."

Congratulations to the young Squire of Tregeare, and to his esteemed and widely-respected parents. Long may he have to wait before we know him as the Squire, and long may he occupy the position when he succeeds to it.

THE YOUNG SQUIRE HONOURED.

COMING-OF-AGE OF MR. JOHN LETHBRIDGE.

PLEASING PRESENTATIONS.

The coming-of-age of Mr. John Edward Baron Lethbridge, eldest son of Mr. E. G. Baron Lethbridge, J.P., of Tregeare, near Launceston, was celebrated on Wednesday, when, in addition to many private presents (including a hunting crop from friends in Laneast other than tenantry, and a silver cigarette box from the household staff at Tregeare), presentations were made of a silver salver by the tenantry and a massive silver loving cup by the inhabitants of Launceston. The Squire had hoped to celebrate the event almost privately, but it had somehow leaked out, and there were several presents, including the following :—

Gun, fishing rod, diamond fox head pin, from Mr. and Mrs. Lethbridge.

Book, "Thoughts on Hunting," from Miss Lethbridge and Mr. James Lethbridge.

Field glasses, from Mrs. Lethbridge, sen.

Cheque, from Miss Amy Lethbridge.

Suit case, from Major Guy Lethbridge.

Book, "The Power of the Dog" from Rev. Hugh C. B. Lethbridge.

Hunting crop, from Col. King, D.S.O.

Pearl studs, from Mrs. A. S. Cope.

Barograph, from Mr. A. S. Cope, R.A.

Gold sovereign purse, from Mrs. Christopher Lethbridge and family.

Gold pencil case, from Miss C. M. Lethbridge.

Edward's eldest son John was also feted when he came of age

166

THE BRIDE AND BRIDEGROOM LEAVING THE CHURCH

Marriage of
John E. B. Lethbridge
July 1928

THE BRIDESMAIDS, BEST MAN, AND USHER

DEATH OF MR. LETHBRIDGE.

Great Friend to the Neighbourhood.

OVER 40 YEARS AS MAGISTRATE AND GUARDIAN.

Few men have been more actively engaged in good work in this part of the country than the late Mr. E. G. Baron Lethbridge, of Tregeare, Laneast, whose death announcement on Tuesday morning shocked the neighbourhood. The passing of this well-known figure was all the more tragic because of its suddenness. Except for a sprained ankle, which had incapacitated him for some days, his health was understood to be normal.

Poor Law Association.

So constant had been Mr. Lethbridge's connection with work in the service of his fellow countrymen that one might almost go on without limitation recording instances of his sacrifice of time and labour to help forward some good cause. However, although his time went in working in so many spheres it was in the administering of the Poor Law that he will be most remembered. In this work all he has done will now never be unfolded and only those who have had his company at the local meetings of the Guardians and for many years his presence on the Board of Governors in connection with the Horwell Grammar School was valued, both because of the soundness of his suggestions and his pleasant disposition, to which many would willingly testify. During the years he occupied this position he saw many changes and recently he had the gratification of seeing the Launceston secondary schools, Dunheved and Horwell, amalgamated, which could not have been pleasantly brought about without the unanimity of the Board of which he was a member.

His concern for the agricultural industry was of the most practical description. As one of the oldest members of the Launceston Agricultural Society he was a regular follower of its activities and on more than one occasion he held the honoured position of President—an honour which was fully in accord with the interest he took in the industry in general. Other offices which had been filled by him included the presidency of the Launceston Cottage Garden Society, and Savings Bank.

His popularity in the hunting field was as great as it was elsewhere and

Part of the long obituary of Edward Galton Baron Lethbridge 1867 - 1932

IN SUNDRY PLACES

Chapter 20 - Departed Glory

The tribute that was accorded Edward Galton Baron Lethbridge on his death was obviously well merited, and was indicative of the genuine respect and high regard the community had for a man who had devoted so much of his time and energy to the welfare of others. It may be that his immersion in public work was his escape route from the great sadness of his domestic life, the knowledge that his son would not succeed him at Tregeare.

As John had grown up he had developed a taste for hunting, and indeed did well in the sport for in 1926 he was appointed Master of the Lamerton Hunt, a position he held for many years. In 1928 John married Olive Edwina Medley-Costin, and she gave birth a year later to Mr David Lethbridge who has inherited a great interest in the history of his family, and who now holds the one and only edition of his great grandmother Millicent's book.

Dorothy sitting in the Billiards Room (now the Dining Room)

But when Edward Galton died it was Dorothy, at the age of forty, who took control of Tregeare and became the pivot of attention. Dorothy never married but soon established herself as a personality in the district and continued many aspects of her father's public work. She also became Chairman of the East-North Cornwall bench of Magistrates, and represented Laneast on the Launceston Rural District Council. One of her main interests was the work of the Red Cross, and she was for many years the local society's Nursing Commandant. She was also for many years a keen supporter of the Girl Guide Movement.

Dorothy had been brought up as a Christian and became a regular worshipper at Laneast Church, as her father had been before her, and she continued the Lethbridge tradition as a member of the Parochial Church Council. Her 'reign' at Tregeare lasted for over forty years and in many respects she became the 'grand dame' of the district. It was not an easy period, for values were changing and income was falling and she was by no means free from financial worries. But she sailed through life in imperialistic style with never a hint of trouble and was regarded by all who knew her as indomitable.

In 1951 after nearly twenty years in control she still had a large estate to administer, and its composition is as shown in the following list

Tregeare Estate 1951	Occupier	Acreage
House and Gardens	Miss D.M.B. Lethbridge	15.384
Private Drive and Roads	Joint	9.371
Home Farm and Cottage	Miss D.M.B. Lethbridge	98.254
Woods	In hand	136.435
Tregeare Farm	F.S. Venning	84.831
Tregeare Farm	W.T. Bluett	81.695
Fennel Farm	J.E. Brendon	82.861
Badgall	W.J. Statton	62.536
Tor Park	S. Fry	65.795
Badgall	F.J. Parnall	38.080
Treglum Mill Land	J.T. Burde	19.576
Sweetwell Farm	J. Francis	93.010
North Lane Farm	L.D. Stoman	58.158
High Hall Farm	E.R. Kelly	161.310
Lidcott	J.T. Gynn	164.017
Coombegate	L.J. Dawe	109.856
Lands	P.J. Pett	28.235
Westdownend	H. Bloye	148.557
Tregeare Down	C. Bloye	3.283
John's Cottage	Mrs New	.858
Cottages	Various Tenants	4.006
Badgall Down	In hand	169.402
Tregeare Down	In hand	124.789
Laneast Down	In hand	318.471
	Total	**2078.77**

Plus seventeen properties in Lambeth and Blackfriars, London.

She achieved the reputation of being a martinet in the house, a stickler for convention, and a passionate advocate of economy. It is said that she instituted a rule of 'lights out' at 10pm, and effectively enforced this by herself throwing the main switch at this hour, only candlelight then being available. When she died, the expression of public regret and sympathy was spontaneous and sincere, and her friends and admirers flocked to her funeral at the little church of St. Sidwell's in Laneast. It was perhaps typical that she herself specified who was to conduct the service and she too chose the spring flowers that decorated the altar. These flowers naturally came from Tregeare which is renowned to this day for the beauty of its floral display in springtime.

Staff on the lawn. It was Piper's job to cut the grass.

Major Jim, who succeeded her, was already seventy nine years old and beginning to feel his age. Exactly what proportion of responsibility of running the estate he had borne under his sister's leadership is not known, for the exact nature of the Trust Deed or his father's Will have not been disclosed, but Jim was quite capable of assuming control. His life had been full of activity, and it may well be that his had been the guiding hand in the running of Tregeare for many years.

Apart from the management of the estate Major Jim's life can be summarised in one word – horses. He loved horses, he lived for horses, and his whole career was bound up in the care and control of horses. From his father, and like his elder brother, he inherited a love of hunting, and at Tregeare with stables full of horses and even a pack of harriers in the kennels behind the house, hunting was very much to the fore and the principal topic of conversation. Possibly under Dorothy's regime gentler pursuits achieved some prominence, and no record has been found of Dorothy actually riding to hounds, though in a household so steeped in the sport it would have been unlikely for her not to have been involved in some way.

Jim joined the first Royal Devon Yeomanry as a horse despatch rider and received his commission in 1914. He had been intending to make farming his career but the outbreak of war had put a stop to that, and in the early years he served instead in the desert. In 1916 he transferred to 20th Hussars and went to France, and at the end of the war was posted to Turkey with the Hussars and spent four years there. During this period he was able to do some racing, both point-to-point, and under N.H. rules, and when he returned to England and was stationed at the Cavalry Barracks in York he was able to continue this sport and achieved several wins, also managing to do a little successful Show jumping.

After a few years in Egypt and several trips to Syria to buy horses for officers he was appointed remount officer for South Devon, his job being to pay regular and frequent visits to all the farms in the area to keep an eye on horses that might be suitable for gunners and the cavalry in the event of war. He also had to keep in touch with all the blacksmiths in the area and it was said of him that in time he got to know every horse in South Devon. In 1937 his remount area was increased to include all of Dorset, Somerset, Devon and Cornwall. This enabled him to live at home and Tregeare became a good centre from which he could exercise his surveillance of available horses in the South west.

He was acknowledged as being an exceptionally fine horseman and from 1932 onwards became increasingly interested in hunter judging. Before his father died Jim and his elder brother Jack were regular dedicated huntsman and it is said that the stables at Tregeare never contained less than nine first class hunters. Altogether he hunted with some forty packs during his lifetime and in 1952 took over the East Cornwall for five seasons. He was still hunting two days a week at the age of seventy three. He became one of the country's leading hunter judges and ultimately could claim to have officiated at every major show both in England and in Ireland.

Jim was highly respected in the South west, particularly in hunting circles, and Tregeare became well known as a result. He was President of the Royal Cornwall Show in 1966 when he was serving as Joint Master of the East Cornwall Hounds, a position his father had held before him. His last few years at Tregeare were rather sad ones, for after Dorothy died he was alone in this large house, looked after by a Housekeeper and Nurse. When he died he was cremated, his ashes and those of his sister, being interred in their parent's grave in Laneast churchyard.

With Jim's death the Lethbridge reign at Tregeare was virtually over. It is true that Tregeare House and a certain amount of land came into the possession of David Lethbridge, but not the money necessary to maintain it, and during the last several years it had been starved of maintenance and was in a pretty poor state. At this point it is necessary to remind ourselves that the present account is the story of Tregeare, and not a history of the Lethbridge family, but the two are inextricably mixed and at this stage the fate of Tregeare is very much bound up with the fate of the family.

By Order of the Exors of the late Major J. C. B. Lethbridge

CATALOGUE

of the major portion of the contents of Tregeare House

TO BE SOLD BY AUCTION

at

THE TOWN HALL
LAUNCESTON

on

Thursday, 29th January, 1981

at 10 a.m.

by

KITTOWS

Auctioneers, Estate Agents and Surveyors

LAUNCESTON

Tel. (0566) 2161

Offices at Callington, Saltash, Plymouth, Liskeard & Torpoint

Every Picture Tells a Story

The stark facts are that Jim died in November 1980, in January 1981 the contents of the house were sold by auction, David and his wife took up residence in an empty house but found it quite impossible to remain, and in September 1982 Tregeare was sold. The Lethbridge Tenure had lasted for exactly one hundred and fifty five years.

During this comparatively short period Tregeare had been built up by careful husbandry and good management into a large and wealthy estate, and three generations had lived off the fat of the land, but in the last fifty years it had all crumbled away until in desperation the remnants had to be sold. So what went wrong?

It could be argued that the seeds of trouble were sown in John Christopher Baron Lethbridge's time. He had inherited a fabulous estate from his father and his lifestyle responded accordingly. Millicent was astute enough to appreciate what was likely to happen, and after her husband's death took courageous action, perhaps the mistake she made was in leaving Edward Galton in charge when he was too young to appreciate the pitfalls.

In many ways Edward was a marvellous man, but he failed to spot the cancer that was already gnawing at the internal structure of this little empire, and his obsession with horses and hunting blinded him to the fact that his lifestyle was no longer economically viable. This was borne out and emphasised by his eldest son, who perhaps did not have the intellectual capacity of his father, and who was devoted to hunting to the exclusion of everything else. The realisation shattered his father and actually drove him to a dramatic change in policy.

The Trust Deed he established was designed to safeguard the lives of his immediate successors but was no instrument for launching a solution to the problem. It was in fact a rearguard action which could only delay the moment of truth. After his death Dorothy and Jim bravely kept the flag flying but it was no use, and when Jim died the end was near.

The real loser in this pathetic game of keeping up appearances was Jack's only son, David. At an early age David managed to alienate the affections of the whole family, simply by not loving horses, and in a household obsessed with the horse this was a cardinal sin. But David wanted to be an engineer and this was the ultimate heresy. When he was still quite small the family tried to convert him, they even went so far as to 'blood' him at the killing of a fox, a savage rite which many people would regard as brutal and unacceptable in this day and age, and David was suitably revolted. He was told that as far as money was concerned it was a case of 'horses or nothing.'

While this was going on the estate steadily deteriorated, the house was neglected and no one seemed to accept any responsibility. Dorothy complained to the Trustees on more than one occasion, and though there was money available for maintenance nothing was done. When Jim died Tregeare House was actually empty for two years with no care or maintenance whatsoever, and it does not need a genius to know what happens to an old house when this occurs. A.L. Rowse saw Tregeare in 1982 and wrote his little poem which is quoted on page forty. He was dead right.

IN SUNDRY PLACES

Chapter 21 - The Sleeping Beauty

In September 1982 Tregeare was bought by Michael Reeve and his wife, and the 'renaissance' began. Michael and Charmian were living in Suffolk seeking a larger country home and in Tregeare they found just what they wanted, though there was much work to be done. On their first visit, as they scrambled over fallen trees and brambles walking up the drive and rounded the bend to see the house, Michael remembers saying to Charmian "What a sleeping beauty". The task before them must have been daunting but they set about it with strong and hopeful hearts, and slowly but steadily order began to be restored. Charmian, skilled in the arts of décor, tackled the inside of the house, while Michael faced the monumental problems connected with keeping out the weather. The spirit of the house stirred and awoke from its sleep.

The aftermath of the fire in 1983

The house in the snow

*The Window commemorating
the building of the house in 1790*

*The Hall and
Front Door*

The magnificent Staircase

Great progress was made, but a year later disaster struck. On 31st December 1983 Charmian woke at 1am hearing a noise, and woke her husband. They were horrified to find that fire had broken out in the attic which was well alight. They phoned the fire brigade and then proceeded to evacuate the children who were taken in at Home Farm by John and Doris Emmett. Hugo was ten and Luke six years old, and this was an excitement in the middle of the night they could have well done without, but thank God for Christian neighbours.

The first fire engine arrived from Lanson in an incredible seventeen minutes, an example of swift service in an emergency that it would be impossible to beat. Fifteen firemen came from Lanson, and ultimately another twenty from Delabole, Bude and Bodmin together with eight appliances. Without them the house would have died. The fire was out by 9am but 1,200,000 gallons of water had been poured on it and the devastation and damage can be imagined. Holes were drilled in the library ceiling and saved its plasterwork from collapse.

What a set back this was for Michael and Charmian who saw so much of their hard and patient work destroyed. Six months went by before repairs could be started, and it was mid-December before they were completed. This was an agonising time for the Reeves, but out of it came goodness. They were so appreciative of the efforts and skill of the firemen that Michael wrote a personal letter of thanks to each of the fifteen Lanson firemen, an action that in this generally ungrateful world must be accorded the highest praise. Later, in May 1985, a Thanksgiving Service was held in which the Bishop of St. Germans gave a blessing. David Lethbridge and his wife Juliette and son Andrew were present.

Michael and Charmian continued their good work and Tregeare remained as their much loved second home for another eleven years, but alas in 1996 the house and estate changed hands again. This could have been a disastrous move for Tregeare, but fortunately it was bought by a man who had already proved that he possessed exceptional skills in the restoring of old houses – and incidentally, though this is another story, in the rebuilding of old wooden boats. Anthony and Daphne Winter came from Kent where they had successfully revived a large and derelict farmhouse together with around sixty five acres of land. They had, between them, just the skills that Tregeare needed, and the determination to apply them. The 'renaissance' was resumed, and at an increased rate. A new roof was fitted and major work was carried out to the fabric of the building in eradicating remaining damp and bringing it up to first class condition.

As an example of the thoroughness of the restoration the Victorian window frames, which were not beautiful, were replaced by frames with glazing bars, replicas of the originals, and the improvement this made to the appearance of the house was staggering. The shades of Jasper Baron and his family must have exulted.

The Reeves had made considerable progress in clearing the grounds but there was still work to be done. In the garden and the grounds the transformation was even more dramatic. There were many trees that had reached the end of their natural life and were in a dangerous condition. A programme of restoration based on the best possible professional advice was instituted and work began on the commercial woodlands and the woodland gardens surrounding the house.

Immediately there was a local public outcry, protest meetings were held in an attempt to stop the new owner felling all these beautiful trees. The County Tree Officer chaired the two meetings that were held, and initially seemed to be on the side of the protesters, but when he appreciated that only unsafe trees were to be felled, and that the work that was being carried out was solely to improve the woodland and prevent accidents, he wisely decided to support it.

In the event the woods were cleared of rubbish, rides were opened up and allowed to grass over, and between four and five thousand new trees were planted in the estate generally. This latter is a staggering figure. In a few years time when maturity has been achieved the woodland garden itself will be amongst the finest in Cornwall. In the open spaces round the new plantings wild flowers, whose seeds had lain dormant for years, have sprung up and already the garden is a demi-paradise. If A.L. Rowse the poet and historian, who loved Cornwall so passionately, could see it now – and who knows, he may be able to – he would surely be constrained to write another verse about Tregeare today. Perhaps he might even approve the little poem on page 182.

Front Door

Rear Entrance

A corner of the Woodland Garden

One of the blue Azaleas

TREGEARE RESURGENT

"Gone are the days when the house stood cold and gaunt,
Now all is warmth and light again,
No longer are the windows vacant eyes
Looking out on weeds and desolation,
No longer are the woodlands choked with brambles,
Nor nettles rampant, bindweed everywhere.
Once more the rides and walks are free,
The laurel hedges trim and neat, the vistas
Pleasing to the eye, the lawns close-cropped,
A fitting background to the rhododendrons.
The trees hold up their heads and breathe again,
And welcome recent plantings; not only trees
But springtime bulbs aplenty.
Once more is heard the happy sound
Of children, young and old together, a family,
And life abounds, inside and out.
The old house hears and positively beams
Its approbation. Once more it smiles
Through eyes new bright with glazing bars.
Proudly it stands. But then –
With all this love and care around
How can a house not sing?

Appendix A - The Tregeare Family Portraits

The following is a list of all portraits sold at auction on Thursday 29 January 1981. Present owners where known are given. Edward Galton Baron Lethbridge, who inherited the Estate in 1885, wrote some interesting comments about some of them, and these are also given. The list is taken from the auctioneers sale catalogue.

1. John Christopher Baron Lethbridge 1839–1885

    18"x14" (oval) Oil on board. Believed to be by Lance Calbin taken from a photograph. Lot No. 361. Sold at auction for £230.

2. Millicent Galton Lethbridge (wife of the above)

    18"x14" (oval) Oil on board. Believed to be by Lance Calbin taken from a photograph. Lot No. 362. Sold at auction for £230.

3. John King Lethbridge 1789-1861

    30"x25" Oil on canvas by W.A.Smith. Lot No. 363. Sold at auction for £70.

4. Emma Palmer 1803-1876 Second wife of John King Lethbridge and on her lap Harriet Anne 1841-1879.

    30"x25" Oil on canvas by W.A.Smith. Lot No. 364. Sold at auction for £200.

5. Christopher Lethbridge 1760-1830

    30"x25" Oil on canvas by Andrew Giddes. Lot No.365. Sold at auction for £150.

6. Mary (Polly Copland) Lethbridge 1759-1825 Wife of Christopher Lethbridge.

    30"x25" Oil on Canvas by Neville Northey Burnard of Altarnun. Lot No. 366. Sold at auction for £200.

7. Rev. Edward Palmer

    35"x27" Oil on canvas. Lot No.367. Sold at auction for £90.

8. Mary Freith Wife of Rev. Edward Palmer.

    36"x28" Oil on canvas. Lot No. 368. Sold at auction for £105.

9. Elizabeth 1837-1844, Emma 1838-1876, John Christopher Baron Lethbridge 1839-1885 and Harriet Anne 1842-1879.

    16"x20" Oil on canvas. Lot. No. 369. Sold at auction for £620.

10. William and Elizabeth Ann Baron

    This portrait has already been described. Painted by Samuel Woodforde R.A. 50"x40" Oil on canvas. Lot No. 370. It was sold at the auction for £3,600 and is the property of Mr Richard Lethbridge of Fulbrook, Oxon.

11.   <u>Elizabeth Ann Baron</u> 1799-1833

1.   A portrait painted by Samuel Woodforde R.A. when she was two or three years old, playing with flowers. 36"x28" Oil on canvas. Sold at auction for £560. Lot No. 371. Now the property of Mr Christopher Lethbridge of Faringdon.

12. 2. A portrait of her as an adult, copied by W.A. Smith from a portrait by Burnard. 32"x26" Edward writes of this one – "This portrait was unfinished and Mrs John King Lethbridge No.2 (Emma Palmer) sat for her hands! The Ruff was added as the artist had made her lovely neck preposterously long! She had two boys who both died in infancy – a charming, lovely and intellectual woman whom my grandfather married eight years before there was any prospect of his inheriting through her the London and Cornish Estates."

Millicent Lethbridge, Edwards mother, also wrote a comment on this painting. She said "One taken after her marriage, in which the face has a very sweet and lovable expression, but somewhat melancholy." Lot No. 372.

Sold at auction for £190 and now the property of Mr Christopher Lethbridge of Faringdon.

Note referring to Portrait 12 by Edward Lethbridge.

"Her great great great great grandfather John Baron of Treludick, Bap:1580, Mar:1607 Johan Sleman of Egloskerry ("Heiress") died 1654. Bought in 1628 a Messuage at South Tregeare of Edward Hawke who in 1576 had bought it of "George Greynvyle" of Penheale Esq., Lord of the Manor – His younger son "Degory" is the first "Baron of Tregeare"."

13.   <u>Jasper Baron</u> 1768-1798

Simply listed in the Sale Catalogue as "Oil on canvas. 36"x26" portrait of Jasper Baron 1768-1798." Fourth child of Oliver Baron and Elizabeth Booth. Sold at auction for £520 and now the property of Mr Richard Lethbridge. Lot No. 373.

Edward Lethbridge does not comment on this picture but writes as follows-

"Born April 28 1768. Married Elizabeth Pearce of Mevagissey May 1794, their children being William and Elizabeth Ann. Died 1798 (aged 30). His wife also died young.

He added the main block of the mansion to existing premises about 1790 the builder being the father of old William Burt of Lanson (who often worked for me). Old Tregeare which I had to pull down and which stood behind the two newer now facing the Village Green with the same iron gates and "wall garden" was also occupied by Barons.

I preserved as relics the oak chairs in the Hall "W.B. 1750" and two others made from the front door etc. with original inscription. Two granite windows introduced into the two side walls at the back. Granite arch and window forming seat at the Pond – being the old front door and dairy windows – Granite steps at the Pond which had formed the sides of the open hearth.

The properties had passed from Oliver (Barrister of the Inner Temple) who died May 20 1786, to his eldest child Oliver who died 1793 and left both estates to his mother (Elizabeth Booth whose portrait exists) she died in 1796 and her fourth child Jasper succeeded. Query: since Jasper died in 1798, was Tregeare built between 1796 and 1798 or begun earlier by his brother or mother?"

14. Ann Baron

Edward Lethbridge writes –

"Daughter of Oliver (of the Inner Temple – Barrister at Law died 1786) and Elizabeth Baron (nee Booth) and sister of Jasper. Born 1764 August Died on the eve of her wedding – her brocaded silk dress being in my possession and worn at a fancy dress Ball by A.D.I.L." (Ada Dorothy Ivy Lethbridge, Edward's wife). This portrait 36"x28" Oil on canvas sold at auction for £400. Lot No. 374.

15. Elizabeth Booth

Edward Lethbridge writes –

"Wife of Oliver married March 8th 1762. Died 1796. Oliver William her son by his will made in 1787 gave the Property to his mother. He died in 1793 aged 30. She left it to her younger son Jasper."

Portrait 36"x28" Oil on canvas sold at auction for £360. Lot No. 375.

16. George Baron 1626-1686

Edward Lethbridge writes –

"8th child of John Baron of Treludick (b.1580) and Joan Sleman. Baptised April 1. 1626. Married Sept. 21 1671 Elizabeth widow of John Howland of Streatham whose daughter Elizabeth married Wriothesley Duke of Bedford. Died without issue April 12 1686.

He settled in London and was a successful merchant. In 1677 he purchased part of the Old Paris Garden Estate from William Angell for £1600.

In 1685 he created the changes on the Property in Great Wood Street for the Cornish Charities, viz Egloskerry Bread Money 1/- a week to be spent in 12 loaves for 12 poor persons. Egloskerry Vicar £10 per annum. Launceston Grammar School £10 per annum. (Each of these I have redeemed.)

In 1722 William of Tregeare (b.1652:m.1677 Margery Dodge: d.Dec 9 1732) whose coffin slate was brought to me when the Baron vault was filled, purchased a further portion of the Estate from William Small. He was George's elder brother Digory of Tregeare's eldest son and grandson of John of Treludick who settled at Tregeare about 1628."

This portrait, oil on canvas, Lot 376 was sold at auction for £250 and is now the property of Mr Percy Uglow of Treludick.

17. William Baron (18th century)

This portrait is believed to be of William Baron. 30"x25" oil on canvas, Lot 377. Edward Lethbridge writes –

"Either this or No. 18 must be William Baron – Oliver's (Inner Temple) Brother. Born May 21 1724. Described by J.K.L. as "dear Elizabeth's great uncle"."

Sold at auction for £180. and now the property of Mr Richard Lethbridge.

18. Portrait of a gentleman

30"x25" oil on canvas, Lot 378. Edward Lethbridge comments "Is this William (as above) or Oliver himself, or Rev. John Baron of Pattishall."

Sold at auction for £100.

19. Anna Maria

Edward says of this one –

"Eldest daughter of Rev. John Baron of Pattishall who was eldest son of Wm. Baron of Tregeare and eldest brother of Digory Baron of Tregeare, the father of Oliver, grandfather of Jasper, great-grandfather of Elizabeth Ann Lethbridge. Anna Maria married (1) Weaver Abley Esq., and (2) Richard Dickenson. (Rev. John b:1681. m:1720. d:1763)"

30"x25" Oil on canvas. Lot No.379.

Sold at auction for £150.

20. Edward Galton Baron Lethbridge 1867-1932

Eldest son of John Christopher Baron Lethbridge and Millicent Galton Lethbridge. 21"x17" Oil on canvas by Sir Arthur S. Cope. Lot No.380. Sold at auction for £120 and now the property of Mr David Lethbridge.

21. Ada Dorothy Ivy Lethbridge

Wife of E.G.B.Lethbridge. 21"x17" Oil on canvas by Sir Arthur S. Cope. Lot 381. Sold at auction for £70 and now the property of Mr David Lethbridge.

22. <u>Edward Galton Baron Lethbridge</u>

Portrait with Harriers, Rough Tor and Brown Willy in the background. 48"x36" Oil canvas by Heywood Hardy R.O.I. Lot 382. Sold at auction for £2,200.

23. <u>Ada Dorothy Ivy Lethbridge</u>

With her three children John, Dorothy and James. 48"x36" Oil on canvas by Heywood Hardy R.O.I. Lot 383. Sold at auction for £1,300.

There are a further twenty one oil paintings listed, four by Sir Arthur S. Cope and four by Charles Branscombe. Most of these paintings are landscapes or seascapes, and in total they fetched at auction another £5,900.

Appendix B - Philip Gidley King

Born No 5 Southgate St., Launceston 23 April 1758, his parents being Philip King a Draper and Eutricia who was the daughter of John Gidley an Attorney of Exeter.

He attended a small boarding school in Yarmouth Isle of Wight from 1765-1770 which prepared boys for entry to Naval Academy. The school was situated in Yarmouth High Street, the site now being a Wine Bar. It was run by a Mr Goodall, or a Mr Bailey, and achieved a reputation for teaching navigation. Capt. William Bligh of the Bounty, Capt. Cook, and Horatio Nelson are all believed to have learned their navigation there. (Goodall ran the school in 1735 when it was first formed, and Bailey was probably the Head in 1765).

Philip Gidley King duly entered the Royal Navy and on 13 May 1787 sailed from the Isle of Wight as First Lieutenant in HMS Sirius, one of the convict ship escorts going to Botany Bay. Arrived January 1788.

In February 1788 King was sent to find a sub-colony on Norfolk Island. He took with him several convicts, men and women, a few free men, a small guard, some farm-yard animals and six months provisions. One of the female convicts, Ann Innet subsequently bore him two sons, Norfolk and Sydney. In 1790 he was sent to London to press the Government for help with the urgent needs of the penal settlement. While in England he met and married Anna Josepha Coombe of Hatherleigh in Devon, was promoted Commander and four days after the wedding was sent back to 'New Holland' as Lieut. Governor of Norfolk Island. Mrs King accepted the situation and the two natural children, and she turned out to be a pillar of strength. They sailed on 15 March 1791.

His health was not good and he was wracked with gout, no doubt because of an inordinate liking for port – he was receiving an annual shipment of thirty six dozen bottles.

In April 1796 King returned to England to seek medical advice and brought his family with him – Philip Parker born 13 December 1791, Anna Maria born 22 April 1793, Utricia born October 1795, Elizabeth, born at sea during the voyage on 10 February 1797.

In 1798 King was appointed Governor of New South Wales and after much delay he with his wife and daughter set sail in September in an unseaworthy ship that had to return almost immediately. It was another fifteen months of frustration before they were able to sail again in December 1799 and this period caused him serious financial hardship as he was not being paid and was living on his savings. At this time the troubles met with in founding a settlement on the other side of the world with more convicts than free men had become an embarrassment to the Government who had hoped to have heard the last of them by now. The Kings arrived in Port Jackson (Sydney) in May 1800 after five months at sea. It was September before King obtained control of the Colony.

He found there was much needed doing to put the community on its feet and to counteract the "vice, dissipation and a strange relaxation which pervaded every class and order of people".

This he did with the help of his wife, very successfully, starting with the children, of whom there were large numbers. Half the population were illegitimate and marriage was at a discount. When the population reached a total of nine thousand there were only three hundred and sixty married couples.

King's reign as Governor came to an end in February 1807 when he handed the Colony over to William Bligh, another Cornishman. He retired to England but his health finally deserted him and he died in September 1808 at the early age of fifty. Such was the tardiness of the Government that he was not yet in receipt of a pension, which seems a poor reward for a man who had served his country faithfully and well for twenty years, often in the most adverse circumstances.

Appendix C - Tregeare Estate in 1839 - 1840

Egloskerry Portion

		A.	**R.**	**P.**
52	East Hill	7	3	37
53	Marsh	2	2	23
54	Middle Hill	6	1	23
55	West Hill	6	3	20
58	Lower and Bove Town	6	2	31
69	Brandise	5	2	10
70	Great Field	10	3	23
71	Bove Town	6		22
72	Little Meadow (Little Penheale)	2	3	10
73	Road and Waste	1	3	30
74	Higher Great Park	5	1	14
75	Silver Park	3	2	9
76	Furze Park	10		1
77	Higher Beevils Down	12		32
78	Plantation (Fir)		1	10
79	Garden		1	39
80	House and Garden			35
81	Yonder Plantation	32	1	27
82	Middle Beevils Down		3	18
82A	Road and Waste	2		24
83	Little Brandises Park	3	1	33
84	Lower Beevils Down	8	2	1
85	Genys Park Marsh	2	2	24
86	Great Genys Park	4	3	4
87	Strap	1		8
88	Great Meadow (Little Penheale)	4	1	29
89	Higher Marsh	1	1	18
90	Middle Marsh	1		35
91	Lower Marsh	1	2	36
92	Cowlards Plantation	1	3	6
93	Little Town Meadow	1	3	10
94	Well Meadow	5	3	15
95	Long Meadow	5		30
96	Dung Field	4	3	12
97	Home Park	6		6
98	Hidden Land	5	1	32
99	Canna Park	8	1	36
100	Park Dove	6		28
101	House and Garden			38
102	Pig House Orchard		1	14
103	Willow Marsh		2	8
104	Great Orchard	1	2	2

			A.	R.	P.
105	Little Park		1	3	14
106	Lane			1	7
107	Mowhay				29
108	Farm yard and houses			2	9
109	Stable Orchard			1	28
110	West Town		3	2	26
111	Coppice		3	2	7
112	Widdows Corner		2		29
112B	Plantation				3
113	Hill		3	2	31
114	High Park		2	2	36
115	Eaver Park		6	1	6
116	Cucks Ball		3	1	36
117	Lower Cucks Ball		6	3	38
118	Cucks Ball Plantation		13		36
119	Treland Meadow		1		17
120	Lower South Park Marsh		2		34
121	South Park Meadow		1	3	13
122	South Park Marsh		1	3	8
123	Thistle Park Marsh		1	1	33
124	Higher South Park		2	1	27
125	South Park		2	1	28
126	Lower South Park		4	3	22
126C	Little Garden				10
127	Swerl		4		28
128	Thistle Park		3		2
129	Higher South Park Arable		1	1	35
130	Higher South Park		3	3	24
131	South Park		3	3	13
132	South Park Meadow		1	2	3
133	Old Park Marsh			3	13
134	Old Park		4	1	9
135	Orchard (Frogapit)		1	16	
136	House and Garden				26
137	Orchard			1	36
138	Tregeare Down Under Down		294		18
139	House and Garden				23
140	Kittows Meadow			3	14
141	Blackland (Frogapit)			2	30
142	Blackland		1		12
143	Lower Blackland		1		23
144	House and Garden				26
145	Blackland		1	3	4
146	Lane Park		2	2	36
147	Home Lane Park		2		36
148	Great Meadow		3	2	7
149	Long Meadow		1	1	11

		A.	R.	P.
150	Long Orchard	2	1	1
151	Higher Peel Park	2		32
152	Lower Peel Park	3		33
153	Lower Stile Park	3		24
154	Dutch Acre		3	29
155	Nettle Bed Orchard	1	10	
156	Bakers Meadow	1		35
157	Bakers Meadow Orchard		1	13
158	Farm Yard and Houses		1	6
159	House and Garden		1	7
160	House and Courtlege			13
161	Mowhay			38
162	Mowhay			32
163	Higher Stile Park	2	1	1
164	Mowhay		3	38
165	Garden			26
166	Barn and Mowhay		1	
167	Waste			12
168	Houses and Waste			22
169	House and Garden			6
170	Higher Bove Town	1	7	5
171	Binland	4		
172	Lower Bove Town	1	1	21
173	Hargates Meadow	1	1	31
174	Stentaway	1		29
175	Stentaway		2	30
176	Bove Town	3		
177	Beacon Park	3	1	33
178	Beacon Park	4		32
179	Outer Binland	3	1	14
180	Smiths		2	5
181	Higher Bovetown			37
182	Binland Garden			23
183	Smiths Park		1	1
184	Garden Orchard		1	23
185	Orchard		1	10
186	Houses and Yard			26
187	Courtlege			7
188	Common and waste in Tregeare road	5	2	38
189	Doctors Meadow	2		14
190	Wilderness Orchard		3	33
191	Garden		1	17
192	Houses Courtlege and Garden		1	
193	House and Two Gardens			15
194	House and Garden			31
195	Garden		3	18
196	Nursery		2	2

		A.	R.	P.
197	Herridge	3	2	31
198	Middle Dinner's Field	3	1	13
199	Dinner's Field	4	1	23
200	Home Bradland	4	2	20
201	Bradland	3	3	8
202	Higher Bradland	4	3	28
203	Bradland	2	3	5
204	Homer Hurdleway	3	3	24
205	Middle Hurdleway	3	3	6
206	Outer Hurdleway	3	1	21
207	Outer Broomhill	8		17
208	Higher Broomhill	2	2	35
209	Lower Broomhill	2	1	37
210	Marsh		3	
211	Lower Broomhill	2	1	28
212	Broomhill	2	3	19
213	Long Broomhill	3	1	22
214	Lower Long Stick	4	2	34
215	Higher Long Stick	3	2	27
216	Little Long Stick	3	3	20
217	Lower Bradland	3	2	39
218	Lower Bradland	3	2	24
219	Lower Bradland	2	1	21
220	Lower Home Bradland	3		1
221	Lower Dinner's Field	3	3	11
222	Herridge	4	1	5
223	North Meadow	2	2	4
224	Dinner's Marsh	4		25
225	Bradland Marsh	1	2	26
226	Bradland Marsh	2		19
227	Lower Bradland Marsh	3	1	36
228	Bradland Marsh	5		25
229	Little Long Stick Marsh	3		7
230	Long Stick Marsh	1		
231	Marsh	1		1

Tregeare Estate in 1840   *Laneast Portion*

	Tresparne	A.	R.	P.
295	Home & Garden			17
296	Henders Garden		2	32
297	Shut Meadow		3	14
298	Cholwell	4	2	25
299	Higher Cholwell	2	3	16
300	Common	4	1	17
301	West Park	2	2	35
302	Homer West Park	1	2	37

		A.	R.	P.
303	Lower West Park	1	1	18
304	Stony Park	1	3	17
305	Mill Ground	4	3	8
306A	Meadow	1	0	3
306	Strap Meadow		3	36
307	Barn Orchard		1	24
308	Croft	2	0	31
309	Long Park	3	3	14
310	Farm Yard	1	2	28
311	Mowhay and Barn			17
312	Garden			22
313	Undertown	1	3	4
314	Higher West Park	1	3	38
315	Middle West Park	1	1	26
316	Lower West Park	3	2	31
317	Strap West Park			
318	Marsh		3	26
319	Lower Undertown	3	1	18
320	Hill	1	2	0
321	Middle Undertown	2	0	32
322	Plain Park	1	2	17
323	Hillhead	4	2	10
324	Green Field and Hill	3	3	26
325	Reed Field	2	3	22
326	Mill Ground	2	0	38
327	Ryland	2	3	0
328	Lower Quarry Park	5	3	23
329	Quarry Park	1	2	1
330	Middle Close	1	3	23
331	Lanny Foot	1	1	23
332	Homer Nicholas Field	1	3	11
333	Meadow	1	2	27
334	House and Garden			33
335	Orchard		2	33
336	Homer Marsh		2	24
337	Outer Marsh	1	0	21
338	Old Orchard	1	0	21
339	Nicholas Field		3	9
340	East Ground Marsh		1	30
341	Great East Ground	7	0	14
342	Homer East Ground	2	0	35
343	Underlane	2	1	5
344	Outer Underlane		1	37
345	Mowhay Plot or Plots	1	1	20
346	Higher West Park		3	34
347	Higher West Park	2	2	11
348	Abovehouse Plot	1	0	16

		A.	R.	P.
349	Abovehouse Plot		3	32
350	Homer East Ground		2	5
351	Great Above Town	7	0	37
352	Little Above Town	1	2	26
353	Homer East Ground	3	2	6
354	Long East Ground	5	0	21
355	Lower East Ground	2	2	6
356	Higher East Ground	2	2	12
357	Down Park	2	2	24
358	Higher East Ground	3	2	3
359	Tresparne Down	13	3	4
	Parmory			
360	House and Garden		2	17
361	Plot		1	38
362	Garden			8
363	Meadow	2	2	19
364	Hill Park	1	3	15
	Tor Park			
420	Garden			10
421	Meadow	1	3	12
422	Three Corners	2	0	8
423	Three Quarters	1	0	31
424	Rock Park	1	2	13
425	Broom Field	2	3	14
426	Long Field	2	0	2
427	Lower Field	1	3	7
428	House and Garden			18
429	Garden			20
430	Doidge's Park	1	1	13
431	Lower Lanna Park	4	1	7
	Bad Gall			
432	Higher Lanna Park	2	0	36
433	Homer Great Field	6	1	26
434	Outer Great Field	8	0	0
435	Homer Farland	4	2	3
436	Middle Farland	5	3	5
437	Three Corners	5	1	23.
438	Stabbage Meadow	2	3	9
439	Middle Lower Field	2	3	24
440	Stabbage Lower Field	2	1	33
441	Mill Park	2	2	12
442	Staffage Marsh	1	2	2
443	West Park Marsh	1	3	20
444	Marsh	1	1	35

		A.	**R.**	**P.**
445	Marsh	1	0	6
446	Lower East Town	3	2	18
447	Lower North Town	2	1	10
448	North Park	2	0	22
449	East Town	2	1	29
450	Mill Park Orchard		1	5
451	Courtlege			30
451A	Mowhay			15
452	Blewetts Meadow		1	17
453	Garden			18
454	Garden			35
455	House and Two Gardens			30
456	Homer Lanend Field	1	3	22
457	Lane End Field	1	2	1
458	Lower Lane End Field	1	0	13
458A	Slip			20
459	Tor Park	3	0	26
460	Lower Cross Park		3	15
461	Higher Cross Park	1	0	13
462	Plot		2	20
463	Green Plot		1	8
464	House and Garden			24
465	Meadow	1	2	28
466	Courtlege			38
467	Shutts Meadow	1	2	22
468	Little Long Plot		1	30
469	Little Long Plot		1	30
470	Garden			7
471	Common Meadow	1	1	18
472	Common Marsh	2	0	0
473	Marsh	1	3	33
474	Great Fieid	3	1	1
475	Little Old Orchard		1	20
476	Ham		3	35
477	Middle Plot	1	1	21
478	Higher Plot	1	0	37
479	Long Plot		3	19
480	Lower Meadow	1	1	10
481	House and Garden			28
482	Abovetown	1	2	4
483	Higher Meadow	1	2	20
484	Garden			16
485	Garden			27
486	Green and Waste	2	2	4

	Tregeare	A.	R.	P.
487	Pleasure Ground	1	0	
488	Courtlege		1	17
489	Plantation	1	3	3
490	Plantation	4	0	9
491	Plantation	2	0	10
492	Underlane	4	2	3
493	Waterlane	2	1	16
494	Higher Broom Hill	2	3	21
495	Homer Broom Hill	1	3	20
496	Middle Broom Hill	5	1	26
497	Broom Hill Meadow	5	3	34
498	Lower Broom Hill	4	0	36
499	Broom Hill Marsh	3	2	18
500	Middle Broom Hill Marsh	1	0	0
501	Great Broom Hill Marsh	3	0	0
502	Plantation		1	8
503	Lower West Park	3	1	29
504	Lower Two Gates	3	1	38
505	Lower Giddyhays	2	1	1
506	Higher West Park	3	2	24
507	Higher Two Gates	3	2	16
508	Salterns Abovelane	1	2	33
	Bad Gall			
509	Higher Meadow	1	0	1
510	Higher Abovelane	1	3	24
511	Lower Abovelane	2	1	38
512	Simmons Meadow	8	2	20
513	New Plantation		3	18
514	High Hall Marsh	4	2	4
515	New Plantation		3	37
	Tregear			
516	Plantation	2	3	32
517	Timber Wood	2	0	19
518	Lawn	8	0	35
519	Strawberry		1	28
520	Drying Plot		2	3
521	Clothes Field	1	1	3
522	Wood and Plantation	1	1	27
523	Plantation	3	1	3
524	Higher Widdens	5	1	26
525	Homer Widdens	11	0	4
526	Lower Widdens	2	0	35
527	Widdens Marsh	6	0	25
528	Widden	6	1	21

	Lidcott	**A.**	**R.**	**P.**
529	Higher Seven Acres	4	0	16
530	Horse(?) Field	5	3	17
531	Five Acres	6	1	30
532	Widdens Hill	8	2	34
533	Pengron Marsh	27	0	38
534	Little Hawkes Ground	2	2	10
535	Three Corners	3	1	19
536	Hawkes Ground	8	2	19
537	Waterland	7	0	16
538	Courtlege		1	24
539	Mowhay			36
540	Farm Yard and Waste	1	0	18
541	Plot		1	36
542	Croft Meadow	2	3	13
543	Abovetown	5	3	26
544	Garden			27
545	Orchard		3	8
546	Barn Park	3	2	24
547	Higher Middle Park	3	1	8
548	Marsh	1	3	28
549	Lane Park	3	0	2
549A	Garden			17
550	Mowhay Meadow	2	0	38
551	Coombe Meadow	2	1	21
552	Coombe Marsh	1	2	10
553	Under Hill	6	3	10
554	Fore Street	4	0	28
555	Hillans	5	1	25
556	Outer Hillans	4	3	0
557	Ellen (?) Marsh	4	0	1
558	Long Marsh	2	3	30
559	Hill Meadow	1	2	24
560	Thorn Meadow	1	1	10
561	Broom Field	5	0	35
562	Long land	7	0	37
563	Thorn Field	5	3	20
564	Little Long Land	3	2	1
565	Rowslands Brake	5	3	30
566	Letcott Coombe	20	3	23
	High Hall			
567	Farm House and Buildings	2	0	3
568	Mowhay		1	18
569	Little Orchard			21
570	Garden			18
571	New Orchard		1	35
572	Little Orchard		2	14

198

		A.	R.	P.
573	Woody	1	1	23
574	Garden			8
575	Marshy	1	0	36
576	Wood and Marsh	1	1	14
577	Long Meadow	2	3	36
578	Lower Quarry Park	2	0	17
579	Higher Quarry Park	2	0	36
580	Potatoe Garden	1	0	8
581	New Orchard		1	38
582	Higher Plot	3	1	4
583	Wood	2	1	22
584	Long Land	5	1	3
585	Plantation	1	0	20
586	Outer Round Meadow	1	2	4
587	Homer Round Meadow	1	2	33
588	Outer Cows Field	5	1	24
589	Homer Cows Field	7	1	18
590	Bakes Park	3	2	0
591	Church Park	4	3	18
592	Pool Meadow	3	2	32
593	North Park	7	3	37
594	Croft	8	1	0
595	Long Field	9	1	0
596	Outer Holmans Ground	8	2	10
597	Homer Holmans Ground	8	1	16
598	Rock Field	9	2	25
599	Lower Rock Field	7	0	23
600	North Marsh	4	3	33
601	North Brake	4	3	14
602	Marsh	6	0	19
603	Brake and Marsh	8	3	20
604	South Brake	4	0	7
605	Road Moor Marsh	4	1	36
606	Bay Park	5	2	12
607	Lower East Town	5	2	34
608	Higher East Town	4	3	27
609	Great Meadow	5	2	37
610	Part of Common	10	3	21
611	Tor Park	58	0	13

Duke's Hill

		A.	R.	P.
411	Garden			26
414	Quillet		1	8
415	House and Garden			9
416	Quillet		1	14
417	Marsh	1	1	4
418	Marsh		1	2
Total Acreage (Summary)		**839**	**0**	**38**

Appendix D - Edward Galton Baron Lethbridge

1867 - 1932

When Mr. Lethbridge came of age in August 1888 a quite lavish and remarkable celebration took place at Tregeare. Festivities went on for several days and were very fully reported in the newspapers, the Launceston News, a full-sized paper, devoting no fewer than six columns to the event. Extracts are given below of some of the Testimonials and Speeches, and these form an extraordinary tribute to an equally extraordinary man.

Festivities at Tregeare. August 1888.

The Monday was marked by a dinner at Tregeare to the tenantry, and Mr. Lethbridge was presented with a silver salver.

Festivities at Tregeare.

COMING OF AGE OF MR. E. G. B. LETHBRIDGE.

MONDAY.

The proceedings opened on Monday evening with a dinner to the tenantry of the genial young squire, which was held in the dining hall of Tregeare. Mr. Edward Galton Baron Lethbridge occupied the chair, and he was supported on either side by his respected mother and sister, and other members of the family, The company also included the Revs. Baring-Gould (Blackheath), H. T. May (Southpetherwin), N. Haly (Laneast), Mr. Christopher Lethbridge and Mr. O. L. Cowlard (trustees), Mr. G. R. Vowler, Mr. E. L. Marsack, and the following tenantry:—Messrs. W. Orchard, Keast, W. Jenkin, E. Jenkin, Johns, Venning, E. Venning, Rich, Jasper, A. Hockin, D. Vosper, F. Vosper, Rogers, W. Davey, T. Davey, Prout, Walters, Popplestone, J. Frayn, Blatchford, R. Jeffry, W. Jeffry, Sandercook, Creeper, Gimblett, Tubb, Hawke, Wickett, Hodge, H. Jenkin.

After a sumptuous repast had been partaken of, Mr. E. G. B. Lethbridge (the Chairman) proposed the toast of the "Queen and the Royal Family." He said he was sure no words of his could enhance or strengthen the enthusiasm with which they as loyal Cornishmen and Cornishwomen would receive so auspicious a toast. They testified to their loyalty by the manner in which they celebrated the Jubilee last year, and no one who saw the fires on Laneast Down could have had a doubt of it. (Applause).

The toast was heartily received, the company singing the first stanza of the National Anthem.

Rev. N. Haly, in proposing the health of their worthy friend, Mr. Lethbridge, said: We have very great pleasure in being met together on this occasion, and, having attained his majority, I have pleasure in handing to Mr. Lethbridge this piece of plate, which has been subscribed for by his tenants, and on behalf of the tenants I should like to read a few words that I have prepared, and which I am sure the tenantry will fully endorse. I shall leave this address with Mr. Lethbridge when I have read it. The following was the address read by the rev. gentleman:

"The Vicar of Laneast, with those who from this time are your tenants, beg that you will accept the salver as a token of the respect and esteem which we feel for you. In making our selection of this presentation our wish has been to offer to you on your coming of age something which we hoped might please you and also be of use to you. We indulge the hope that to your friends it will be a source of pleasure to look upon the salver as a proof of our confidence in you as a landlord. We wish to assure you that we value very highly your residence among us as a friend, and that our earnest wish is that by the blessing of Almighty God your life will be spared, and that it may prove a long, happy, and a useful one." (Loud applause).

On Tuesday another dinner at Tregeare and the presentation of a silver claret jug from the tradesmen of Launceston.

To
EDWARD GALTON BARON LETHBRIDGE, Esq.

We, the undersigned, beg to offer to you our hearty congratulations on the occasion of your coming of age.

We trust that you will long live to enjoy the property of which you this day come into possession; and hope that every blessing will richly fall on you and yours in your future career.

We would add that our pleasure in congratulating you on coming into the possession of your Ancestral Home is heightened by the remembrance of the high character of your late Father and Grandfather who were greatly esteemed and beloved by all who knew them.

We beg most respectfully to ask you to accept from us on this auspicious day the accompanying "Silver Claret Jug" as a small tribute in token of our respect and esteem.

Dated this 12th day of August, 1888.

The following were the signatures appended :— John Brimmell, William Burt, William Bate, Edward Bloxsome, George Burt, Charles Ball, Ching & Son, Frederick Couch, Charles Parsons, William Prockter, Brendon Parsons, Edward Pethybridge, P. J. Raddall, Henry Short, Thomas Shearm, jun., William H. Symons, John Henry Cory, William S. Cater, Frederick Downing, Frederick T. Francis, Richard Geake, Charles Hayman, John Hawkins, J. & H. Hender, William Hare, John G. Millman, John Oliver, William Slee, Cyrus Sambolls, James Treleaven, Thomas P. Trood, William Vosper, George Vivian, John Vickery, Robert Wevill, Thomas White, William Wise, Alfred G. Weumoth.

Mr. H. Short said : Mr. Lethbridge, ladies and gentlemen,—As I have known your family all my life time, I may be pardoned for saying a few words on the present occasion. In the first instance I would beg you distinctly to understand sir, that the 38 names, attached to that address are not all the friends you have in Launceston. Had the testimonial been generally known and not having been done on the quiet as it has been there would have been instead of 38 names at least 238. Well, sir, in my younger days I was brought much into contact with your late grandfather, in magisterial and other business. I received very much kindness from him and many lessons of good sound advice. It was with pride and pleasure that I have seen him year after year presiding at the court of Quarter Session, and I hesitate not to say that not one of Her Majesty's judges whoever sat on the Judicial Bench ever presided over cases with greater skill and ability than did your late grandfather, who we used to call our Mr. Lethbridge. Then, sir, your dear father also took an active part in public matters, as Magistrate, as Chairman of the Highway Board, as Chairman of the Board of Guardians, as High Sheriff of the County, and in many other ways made himself generally useful, and endeared himself to every one who had the pleasure of making his acquaintance, and when in the prime of life, to us in the mysterious providence of God he was taken from us, he died not having an enemy on earth, but as regards friends their name is Legion, old and young, rich and poor, one and all grieved, because they had lost a friend. When the late Prince Consort died the nation mourned and he was styled Albert the Good, and what was said of the late Prince Consort, might justly, and with equal truth be said of your late dear father Baron Lethbridge the good. Some years since it was part of my duty annually to come to Tregeare to transact business with him and I well remember an incident which occurred 19 or 20 years ago, after we had done our business your father said, "Now Short you must see the boy," I had not long to wait before your father reappeared with you in his arms. Many of us know a father's pride over his first born, and holding you up he said, "there isn't he a fine fellow." I need scarcely say that I not only acquiesced in his view that you were a fine fellow but said you were a model of a boy—a perfect gem—and what I thought of you as a boy of 12 months I think of you now, sir, as a man of 21 years. A short time since it was my privilege to listen to what I believe was your public maiden speech, and I must say that you acquitted yourself well and delighted your audience, and I thought if the late Lord Beaconsfield when Mr. Disraeli made such a bungle over his first attempt at speech making, and afterwards became Prime Minister of England, who's to say what the present squire of Tregeare may yet become. Yes you have now a wide sphere of usefulness before you and a responsibility as well, but I doubt not from the advice and instruction you received from your dear father, from the home influence and early impressions made on your mind by an affectionate, devoted, and one of the best of mothers, you will discharge every duty that may devolve on you in the same way your predecessors have done. I must heartily congratulate you on your coming of age, and earnestly pray that your life may be long, prosperous, and happy, and that the name of Lethbridge, of Tregeare, may continue to be honoured and adored as long as time shall last. (Applause).

Wednesday was the 'popular' day, and a Reception was held on the lawn for the parishioners of Egloskerry and Laneast, and Mr. Lethbridge was presented with a clock from Laneast and a silver flask and horn from Egloskerry. Tea was served in a marquee.

Thursday saw a Grand Ball being held, and on Friday the servants and orkmen were entertained.

MARRIAGE OF E. G. B. LETHBRIDGE, ESQ.

TREGEARE HOUSE.

THE WEDDING.

The grand parish church of St. John the Evangelist, Torquay, was filled on Tuesday afternoon with a large and fashionable congregation assembled to witness the marriage of Mr. Edward Galton Baron Lethbridge, eldest son of the late Mr. J. C. Baron Lethbridge, of Tregeare, Launceston, and Miss Ada Dorothy Ivy King, younger daughter of the late Rev. Edward King, vicar of Werrington, and seldom has a nuptial ceremony been performed in the beautiful edifice of a more attractive and pleasing nature. The brilliant sunshine streaming through the coloured windows, the chaste floral decorations of chancel and altar adding to the beauty of the scene, whilst additional brightness was imparted by the flowers carried in great profusion by the lady guests. Since the death of her father the bride has resided at Torquay, but both bride and bridegroom and their families are well-known and highly respected in this locality, with which their families have been long and honourably connected. The decease of the parents of bride and bridegroom occasioned alike general regret in the neighbourhood. The late Mr. J. C. Baron Lethbridge will long be remembered as Chairman of the County Magistrates, the Highway Board, and the Board of Guardians, and as a gentleman of the utmost generosity and geniality of character, traits which also find place in his son's life, and the Rev. Edward King was vicar of Werrington for about ten years, previous to which he was curate for several years to the Rev. W. M. Birch (vicar of Ashburton), when he was the vicar of Launceston.

Gibson Weekly Times July 13. 1889

WELCOME HOME TO MR. AND MRS. LETHBRIDGE.

True and hearty welcome was given by the parishioners of Egloskerry and tenantry of Tregeare to Mr. and Mrs. Lethbridge on Tuesday last, on the occasion of "Home Coming" from their wedding tour. The happy pair arrived at Launceston by the 5.29 S.W. Train, and were met by Millman's Greys, which soon brought them in sight of the Union Jack which fluttered a welcome from the Church tower. On nearing the village, the bride and bridegroom were met by about forty gentlemen on horseback, and hundreds of men, women, and children on foot, headed by the Alternun Brass Band, giving music to the tune of "Auld Lang Syne." Flags were flying from house to house across the village, and two noble arches were erected, bearing the mottoes "Welcome Home" and "God Bless You Both." The procession halted in the centre of the village, and the following Address from the parishioners was read by the Vicar, the Rev S. Evans:—

"We, the Parishioners of Egloskerry, rejoice at the opportunity afforded us by your home-coming this day to offer you our very sincere congratulations on the auspicious and happy event of your marriage. We earnestly trust a long period of health and every possible happiness may be yours, and in heartily welcoming you amongst us on your return, we pray that Almighty God may have you both in His holy keeping."

In replying, Mr. Lethbridge said he could not find words to express the pleasure he felt at the hearty reception that day given to Mrs. Lethbridge and himself. He wished them to remember that in bringing home a wife he had not brought a stranger, —for they had known her for a long time,—and he could assure them that she had the welfare of the whole neighbourhood near at heart. Twenty-three years ago about this time, his beloved father stood in a similar position to that in which he (the speaker) now stood, and he trusted that the good example shewn by his dear father and mother would be followed by both himself and wife.

Hearty cheers were then given, and the joyous crowd marched on to Tregeare. A splendid arch to celebrate the occasion was erected at Badharlick, bearing the motto "Long Life and Happiness," and decked with flowers looked very pretty indeed. At Tregeare the scene, says a correspondent, was enchanting—the people cheering, flags flying, the entrance arch bearing the motto "Home, sweet Home," and the Band playing music to the same. An affectionate address was prepared by the Rev. N. Haly for the parishioners of Laneast, and read by Mr. Wm. Jenkins, the oldest tenant, in the absence of Mr. Haly, who was too unwell to be present.

Altogether it was an enjoyable evening, and to see the affectionate and smiling faces of the happy pair as they hastened to shake hands with all around them was a sight not soon to be forgotten. Refreshments in abundance were provided for all who took part in the procession.

WELCOME HOME TO MR. AND MRS. LETHBRIDGE.

A true and hearty welcome was given Mr. and Mrs. Baron Lethbridge on Tuesday, on the occasion of their return from their wedding tour. Very early in the morning parties were very busy erecting arches and continued at the work very pluckily during a regular downpour of rain. One arch was erected opposite the Egloskerry church at the entrance to the village, having a motto "Welcome Home"; another stood at the turning leading to Tregare, with a motto "God bless you both." The Union Jack was flying from the tower and several other flags floated from the tops of arches and across the highway. At Badharlick there was a very pretty arch, displaying a lovely lot of flowers and having a motto "Long life and happiness." At the entrance gate to Tregare House was another well-made arch, with a motto "Home, sweet Home." Mr. and Mrs. Lethbridge reached Launceston by the 5.29 p.m. train, S.W.R. Mr. Millman had waiting a pair of greys, and the party arrived at Egloskerry about 6.0 p.m. Over 40 gentlemen on horseback and hundreds of men, women, and children on foot awaited their arrival. A short distance out of the village on the Launceston road, as soon as they were seen coming, the tenantry formed in procession, headed by the Alternun Brass Band, who immediately struck up "Auld Lang Syne." All on horseback (except tenants) with men, women, and children came behind the carriage. When the village was reached there was a halt, and the following address was read and presented by the Rev. W. S. Sloane Evans, vicar of the parish.—"A true and hearty welcome from the parishioners of Egloskerry, to Mr. and Mrs. Baron Lethbridge on the occasion of home-coming from their wedding tour. We, the parishioners of Egloskerry, rejoice at the opportunity afforded us by your home-coming this day, to offer you our very sincere congratulations on the auspicious and happy event of your marriage. We earnestly trust that a long period of health and every possible happiness may be yours, and in heartily welcoming you amongst us on your return, we pray that Almighty God may have you both in His holy keeping. Signed on behalf of the parishioners this 9th day of July, 1889, W. Sloane Evans, vicar; W. D. Keast, vicar's warden; T. Stenlake, parish warden." Mr. Lethbridge replied by thanking all present in a few well chosen words, after which cheers were freely given and continued until the happy pair were out of sound, the horsemen breaking into a smart trot, leaving those on foot far behind. However, the greater part of those who had assembled at Egloskerry proceeded to Tregare. Another address was here prepared by the Rev. H. Haly, vicar of Laneast, and presented to Mr. and Mrs. Lethbridge by Mr. William Jenkin (their oldest tenant.) A suitable reply was made, after which Mr. and Mrs. Lethbridge left their carriage and entered their home, amid hearty and prolonged cheers. Shortly afterwards Mr. and Mrs. Lethbridge re-appeared and were very busy for a short time shaking hands with all those assembled. There was a very liberal supply of refreshments.

LETHBRIDGE HARRIERS.

A PRESENTATION TO THE MASTER.

Mr. E. G. Baron Lethbridge's ninth season as master of the harriers bearing his name, was marked by a presentation. Of the presentation committee, Mr. Sampson Pearn was chairman ; and Mr. G. Sandercock, secretary. Two hundred supporters and followers subscribed, and at the suggestion of Colonel A. B. Collier, it was decided that the presentation should be an oil painting which was entrusted to his friend, the well-known animal painter, Mr. Heywood Hardy. The picture represents Mr. Lethbridge in his hunting habiliments, standing in a familiar attitude on a piece of moorland rising ground, with Rough Tor and Brown Willy in the distance. The Master is holding in one hand a whip, and in the other a horn. Around him are some of his harriers and at his feet a hare. In the background a mounted attendant is holding the master's horse. Mr. Lethbridge's likeness is faithfully reproduced, and the harriers are easily recognisable as those of the hunt. The colouring is excellent. A tablet on the gold frame bears the following inscription :—" Presented to E. G. Baron Lethbridge, Esq., at the commencement of his ninth season by 200 supporters and followers of his harriers, November 11th, 1896."

The presentation was made at Launceston yesterday, and was preceded by a dinner, to which ninety sat down. Colonel the Hon. CHARLES BYNG presided, and amongst those present were the Mayor of Launceston (Mr. T. P. Trood), Colonel Collier, Dr. T. W. Shepherd, Messrs. J. Kittow, J. D. Dingle (Darley), J. Parnell, J.P., C. R. G. Grylls, C. L. Cowlard, C.C., Rundle Brendon, G. Lobb, C. Parsons, and G. K. Vowler. After the loyal toasts,

The CHAIRMAN said the thought which led to their meeting that day was an extremely happy one, and occurred in the happiest of all places—the hunting field. Everyone was unanimous in feeling that Mr. Lethbridge's sportsman-like conduct deserve their recognition, and even ladies had subscribed to the fund. As for Mr. Lethbridge's harriers, where could they see better turned out or hunted ? He asked the Master to accept the picture, and hoped he would be spared very long to see it hang upon the walls of his house.

The company then drank Mr. Lethbridge's health, and lustily sang " For he's a jolly good fellow," and gave rounds of cheers.

Mr. LETHBRIDGE thanked his friends most heartily for presenting him with such a very handsome picture. He was at first rather sorry they were going to confer such an honour upon him, because he thought if he kept on as Master a few years longer and then gave up they might then give him some little souvenir if they thought fit. However, when he found how well they had responded he sank any objections he had. He could not have been more pleased with the picture. The artist had taken great trouble over his work, spending considerable time amongst the scenery and with the dogs to obtain a true picture. The Mastership of a pack of harriers was not all beer and skittles. There were many difficulties to overcome, which made the good feeling shewn towards him all the more acceptable. During the nine years he had had the harriers he had made few enemies, having done his best to avoid doing so. Mr. Lethbridge then amusingly described the various classes of folk which the huntsman met with in his sport, expressing sympathy with those few farmers who, in keeping them out of their fields, were no doubt sore at having had their property damaged. Speaking of the great enjoyment which was to be got from the hunt, he said if only people who shot hares and obtained 3s. for one could realise the pleasure of the hunt they would never shoot another. Considering the bad times for farmers, he all the more appreciated the kindness which had prompted that class to subscribe so largely to the testimonial. He had great pleasure in proposing the health of "The owners and occupiers of land," who had always, as a class, extended the greatest kindness to them. In some few ways harriers were better than fox - hounds, although undoubtedly the latter were the leading sport. Harriers, however, met a want, there being plenty of men who could enjoy a run with harriers, who could not keep up with foxhounds. He, therefore, considered harriers a farmers' pack. (Applause.)

Mr. J. PARNELL, in reply, hoped Mr. Lethbridge would continue to shew the interest in the sport he had in the past.—Messrs. D. Baker, E. Kneebone, and F. Rickard also replied.

Colonel A. B. COLLIER, in proposing "The Committee," said the 200 subscribers had been only too glad to join in the testimonial.—Mr. S. PEARN, responding, said the manner in which support had been given the presentation had exceeded their most sanguine expectations. To its success the secretary had contributed a great deal, and he, therefore, proposed his health. — Mr. G. SANDERCOCK briefly replied.

Our Weekly Portrait.

MR. E. G. BARON LETHBRIDGE, J.P

In a brief biographical sketch it is difficult to do justice to all that has been done, and is still being done, in the district in which he is such a popular resident, by Mr. E. G. Baron

Lethbridge, of Tregeare. Mr. Lethbridge is not yet 40 years of age, having been born on August 12th, 1867, but despite this fact he is now one of the most prominent and valued public men in the locality. He is the eldest son of the late Mr. John Christopher Baron Lethbridge, J.P., D.L., who was High Sheriff of Cornwall in 1874 ; and, to go farther back still, it is interesting to note that his grandfather was Chairman of the Quarter Sessions for no less a period than 20 years. The subject of the present sketch was educated at Charterhouse, and at St. John's College, Oxford, and in 1888, on the occasion of his coming of age, he received presentations from the townspeople and tenantry. A year later he married a daughter of the Rev. Edward King, Vicar of Werrington, the alliance of two such honoured names being made the occasion of widespread rejoicings and felicitations. In the year of his marriage the honour of a county magistracy was bestowed on him, and for about the same time he has been a member of the Launceston Board of Guardians, his work on this body giving evidence of practical sympathy with the poor, combined with a due regard for the

Royal Cornwall Show.   June 1926.

The President of the Society (Mr. E. G. Baron Lethbridge), who was supported by the Mayors of Launceston and other Cornish boroughs, and Mr. A. M. Williams, M.P. for the Division, formally opening the show.—"Western Morning News" Photo.

THE ROYAL CORNWALL SHOW HELD AT LAUNCESTON

The Mayor of Launceston (left, in chain of office) and Mr. E. G. Baron Lethbridge (in bowler hat), the president, who opened the Royal Cornwall show.

Index